With blessings

Sue Patton Thoele

The

Woman's
Book

······ *of* ······

SOUL

This special hardcover edition is a collection
of the best daily meditations from
Sue Patton Thoele's bestselling series:

The Woman's Book of Courage
The Woman's Book of Confidence
The Woman's Book of Spirit

So vast is the nature of spirit that the energies which flow into it can never fill it, nor those which flow from it exhaust it.

Contents

Foreword

. . . .

I HAVE A CONFESSION. I'M FORGETFUL, I FORGET
school forms, my sister-in-law's birthday, car keys,
church meetings, and to tell my husband (who is
the cook in our household) that friends are coming to dinner. I'm always meaning to get one of
those thick official looking organizers that
promise redemption from guilt and forgotten
meetings but I never seem to get around to it.

Instead of an organizer, I reach for Sue's meditations. Because I'm also forgetful on a deeper and
ultimately more damaging level than dinner parties and bake sales. I forget that I am a lovable,
capable, talented woman. I forget that I am doing
the best I can in each (okay, most) moments. I forget to forgive myself for forgetting. For being less
than perfect. For being funky, prickly, awkward,
unpolished me. I forget that I am a spiritual being
clothed in creaky flesh, that I can choose to do
only those things that contribute healing and
meaning to my life.

This is why I read Sue's meditations. They function as petite alarm clock angels, gently waking
me to the reality that I am filled with, if not infinite
then definitely lavish, possibilities. That I am creative, courageous, and even (gulp) a continually

unfolding miracle. Sue reminds me that "God waits for us by the gates of gratitude." In reading her words, I see the magnificence hidden in the grind of everyday life. I am gently prodded to be present to it, and through this, to my best self.

We all need daily reminders. As I wrote at the end of *The Woman's Retreat Book*, "I see a phenomenon happening in the world of spiritual guidance. The eternal truths are emerging, over and over again, in different yet equally urgent forms. Maybe God is desperately trying to send each of us the same information, packaged in a way that we can grasp (and be grasped by). Each book, video, and teacher seem to be saying similar things." Sue is one of the many amazing teachers available to us, each one prompting us to slow down. Breathe. Listen to your inner wisdom. Act from that wisdom when you can. Above all, choose to be kind to yourself. Choose healing and meaning.

But, thank God, Sue is not all sweetness and light. Like all sincere teachers, Sue reveals how she grapples with the sticky side of life. These meditations do not portray the task of being kind to ourselves in a pat or syrupy manner. We are not told to turn our backs on our gloom, our failings, on life's mysteries that have no answers. Instead, we are inspired to sit with these excruciating feelings. To stare into the cold steel pit of fear. To call on our courage and resolve with Sue's compassionate voice accompanying us as we face our itchy and imperfectly healed wounds.

Why is it so difficult for me, perhaps for most of us, to choose to do what is best for ourselves? To practice loving self-kindness? Why is it easier to be mean to ourselves? I don't know the answer, although it makes me wonder if this isn't the elemental struggle between good and evil, right at the very door of our souls: how we treat ourselves.

I don't know why we flagellate ourselves, why we persist in being less than we are capable of. All I know for sure is this constant practice of remembering offers me hope, a trail of bread crumbs through the maze of my life. Sue Patton Thoele's words, along with other reminders, help me to do this. I can be reminded, each day, to choose life, to choose self-acceptance, to choose healing and meaning.

My challenge, our challenge, lies in remembering to make the choice.

—Jennifer Louden, author of *The Woman's Retreat Book* and *The Comfort Book for Women*

The Treasure Within

WHILE VACATIONING ON THE BAHAMIAN island of Bimini this summer, I received word that my "little" sister—and only sibling—had died unexpectedly. Shocked and saddened, I wandered the beach, feeling incredibly thankful that my husband and I had made a trip to see her and her husband just six weeks before.

But because she had found life so difficult, I was also beseeching God, and whatever angels were listening, to give me a sign that Gayle could now find the peace that had eluded her from a very young age. Very soon after that prayer wafted from my heart, I came upon a conch shell broken in the same way as the one so beautifully rendered on the front cover of this book. Through the hole in its external shell, the burnished pinkness of the conch's inner core shone softly. With tears gently trickling down my face, I felt that I had received a message. A message pertinent to each of us: That, no matter how crusty our outer shells may appear, there remains within us the treasure of an unblemished soul.

The Woman's Book of Soul is a compilation of spiritual segments gleaned from my three previous meditation books, *The Woman's Book of Courage, The Woman's Book of Confidence,* and *The Woman's Book of*

Spirit. It is my hope that reading it will help you see through the shell of your humanness into the luminosity of your soul. As we recognize and tap into the essence within ourselves, we can become profound instruments of healing, able to flood ourselves and others with the light of love and acceptance. Our world, shadowed in pain and ignorance, is in dire need of the grace derived from such tenderness.

Possibly because women have the capacity to conceive and nurture life within us, we have a natural inclination toward relationship and living from our hearts. Because of this, we carry the keys to imparting the grace of heartfelt love and creating a more gentle and healthy society and planet. Although definitely not easy for many of us, in order to become the best models for, and teachers of, love and acceptance, we must first learn to nurture a loving relationship with ourselves. An integral part of such a self-honoring relationship is the ability to mine the treasures of our own souls, to hear and heed the urging of our hearts. That still, small, and infinitely wise voice within.

Hopefully, *The Woman's Book of Soul* can become one of your guides along the spiritual journey of ever increasing connection with heart and soul. It can serve in a number of ways—as a meditation guide, a daily friend, or to find the answer to a specific question. You may want to use it as a powerful intuitive exercise by opening it at random after holding it to your heart and asking your inner wisdom to guide you to the perfect, right entry for you at this moment.

As we surge toward the new millennium, all of us, men and women alike, are called to break free from our shells of fear and self-recrimination and birth a more soulful way of being, create a more spiritually harmonious way to live, and to open our hearts in order to spread love, compassion, care, and healing. Each of us is also called to walk with her sisters and brothers along the way, providing support, guidance, acceptance, encouragement, inspiration, and love.

Re-Greening
Arid Places

*It's essential that we understand that
taking care of the planet will be done as we
take care of ourselves. You know that you
can't really make much of a difference in
things until you change yourself.*

—Alice Walker

THE GREAT ELEVENTH-CENTURY CHRISTIAN mystic, scholar, and physician Hildegaard of Bingen defined sin as spiritual dry-rot, aridity, and refusal to grow. She believed that the opposite of sin was to be gloriously and outrageously alive—green and moist, like nature. Water, a common metaphor for both spirit and femininity, is our most obvious greening agent. In order to grow into the beautiful women we were created to be, we must pour the waters of spirit upon our arid places.

All of us have draught-ridden areas within us that need watering and reclamation. The wonderful news is that even a desert wasteland can be turned into a lush oasis when irrigated with enough water and planted with the right seeds. The same is true of us. No matter how dry or barren some aspects of ourselves or our lives may feel, they can be reclaimed when sanctified by the powerful feminine waters of compassion, forgiveness, right thought, acceptance, and gentle guidance.

Paying Attention to Your Soul's Garden

. . . .

PLANTS ARE WONDERFUL SPIRITUAL TEACHERS.
When we pay attention to their simple needs, they
respond by growing and bringing beauty and life-
giving oxygen into our presence. Plants silently
make us aware of their needs by wilting, yellowing,
or failing to thrive. Equally silent, but often less
obvious, our soul-needs can go unnoticed for long
periods of time. If the needs of our spiritual self are
ignored too long, drought conditions occur, leaving us feeling dried up and lifeless.

Luckily, both flowers and spirits are very
resilient and respond beautifully to a little nurturance. Recently, I was all wrapped up in my work
and totally forgot that my potted geraniums and
impatiens were sweltering in a heat wave. By the
time I noticed them, the impatiens were already
crispy. Plying them with fervent apologies and
much needed water, I urged them to revive. Miraculously, they did. Given a little attention and tender loving care, our spirits are just as forgiving and
equally as anxious to re-green and bloom as were
my flowers.

What does your soul garden look like? Are the
plants and flowers green and happy? If not, what

will quench their thirst? What attention do they crave? What tiny little step can you take right now? What miniature bloom can you attend to soon?

When you listen attentively, you'll know how best to serve your soul's needs. It's very important, however, that we don't try to do too much at once or we set ourselves up for failure and become discouraged. When we consistently sow one small seed, water a single vase, till a square inch of soil, the entire garden reaps the benefit. Taking little soul-seconds—one small prayer, a few-minute meditation, a short burst of gratitude while appreciating nature—helps immeasurably to revive our thirsty spirits.

We don't have to join a convent or live in a cave to attend to our souls, although I admit that it sounds appealing sometimes. Luckily, our souls flower and grow when nurtured with consistent rays of attention interspersed among the busy hours of our days.

I pay attention to the needs of my spirit.
I make time to quench my soul's thirst.

Loving Self to Life

. . . .

AS WOMEN, WE'RE OFTEN TRAINED TO LOVE others a lot, and ourselves a little. Unfortunately this is a backward concept because we're better able to love others when we first love ourselves. I know this idea has been harped on, but that's because it is absolutely true and truth deserves a little harp serenade. Just because the idea of self-love is widely accepted doesn't mean it's easy to do. But no matter how hard it may be for us to practice, it is essential, because lack of self-love and acceptance is the basis for most emotional problems, including the feelings of lifelessness and depression that plague so many women.

Fundamentally, loving ourselves is the best way to re-green our lives into the luxurious and creative lushness that we deserve. Unfortunately, there is no quick-fix, easy answer as to how to do this. Some of us were lucky enough to be taught to love ourselves when we were kids, but, for the rest of us, commitment to loving ourselves and a hundred daily decisions to "take ourselves to heart" are the only ways I've found that work. And they are by no means instantaneous. That's why I firmly believe that becoming consistently and compassionately self-loving is one of our lifelong spiritual tasks.

It seems easiest for most women to begin the

self-loving process by loving their younger selves first. Picturing the little girls we were at about three years old and then showering them with the love that they needed and deserved is a great place to start. If you can't bring yourself to love this little one, call in a marvelously maternal and loving being to cherish and cuddle her for you. When I feel especially needy, I hug a large teddy bear and pretend that it's the "little Susie" inside me who feels unloved or unlovable.

Since love is the only energy that brings lasting change, our sacred charge is to love ourselves to life.

I am loveable.

Each day it becomes easier for me to love myself.

Keeping Anger Moist and Movable

ANGER IS AN OUT-OF-HEART EXPERIENCE. THAT
doesn't mean that it's a terrible no-no and that we
shouldn't feel it or express it.

In fact, examined anger is often an incredible
teacher. Exploring our experience of anger nonjudgmentally often helps us uncover valuable clues
as to what we expect, what we want, what we fear,
and where we feel especially vulnerable. Indeed,
examined anger is a spiritual ally. Examined anger
remains moist and movable, supple and malleable
to our inquiring minds. From it, we can learn to
stop accepting the unacceptable in terms of treatment directed toward us.

However, unexamined and consequently sup-
pressed or repressed anger is a different story. Very
often it solidifies into resentment which shuts
down our hearts and leeches all joy from our lives.
In effect, resentment holds a gun to our heart and
says, "Beware! You better dry up, and protect yourself. Opening up is dangerous." Resentment almost
always guarantees aridity.

I don't know about you, but I was vigorously
trained in anger-aversion and was an apt student.
One of my primary life lessons continues to be transforming my self-loathing and self-judgment whenever I feel anger, and learning to use it constructively.

One great way I've found to keep anger moist and movable is to take it less seriously. Anger is great fodder for humor, and when expressed as such, we're often able to lighten up and laugh. For example, after an incredibly unfair divorce settlement, a friend of ours had Gene and I doubled over with laughter as he expounded dramatically about the book he was going to write: *How to Hold onto Your Anger When It's All You've Got Left!* Through humor, he was healthfully expressing just how upset he was at the injustice of his divorce. His intention was to learn from and move through his anger, but for now, it was giving him the energy he needed to walk this piece of the road.

Give yourself permission to explore and express your anger lightly and from the heart. As the saying goes, "What does it matter if a teaspoon of vinegar is spilled on a hill of sugar?"

I take my anger lightly.
I examine my anger and learn from it.

De-Idealizing Expectations

. . . .

A WOMAN I ADMIRE ONCE COMPLIMENTED ME by saying, "Nowhere in your books did I find a shred of judgment." Luckily, my books are edited, but unfortunately my life is not. Judgment is an ongoing issue for me and for most of my clients.

Judgment arises when our expectations are not met, but often our expectations are idealized and unattainable and, therefore, impossible to meet. When I have gone deeply into examining my tendency to judge, I've found at the root, a set of impossible standards that I hold myself to, which inhibit my ability to love myself and others. Self-judgment gives rise to judgment of others—and both suck the love-enhancing moisture right out of our hearts and create draught conditions in our relationships.

Jamie was going through a very rough period in her marriage and was judging herself harshly for not being able to remain a calm and totally loving parent at all times. From my point of view, she was doing a great job under difficult circumstances. Her husband was in the military and virtually never home, her own emotions were in an uproar, and her sense of security in their future together was teetering precariously. Then, one day, a friend commented to her, "To love perfection is to hate life," which affected Jamie deeply. This profound little sentence helped her understand, at a gut level, what a burden she was placing on herself by expecting perfection in a far from perfect situation.

Although it was not easy for her, Jamie sought therapy and began learning the skills for de-idealizing her expectations and concentrating on self-acceptance rather than self-judgment. Over time the results of her work led to a greater tolerance of her imperfections, an increased ability to flow with life, more relaxed kids, and a revitalized marriage.

As human beings, we are evolving, maturing, and changing continually. It is unrealistic and discouraging to expect perfection from ourselves or others. Letting go of unrealistic ideals frees us to love more and, ironically enough, allows us to be better people.

I love life, imperfections and all.
I love myself, imperfections and all.

Fostering Self-Forgiveness

ONE OF THE MOST EFFECTIVE WAYS TO BLEED our spirit-energy away is to impale ourselves on the twin swords of blame and nonforgiveness. Therefore, the ability to forgive ourselves is essential to our soul's growth. Forgiveness originally meant "to return good treatment for ill usage," which reminds me of a beautiful saying: "Forgiveness is the fragrance the violet sheds on the hand that has crushed it."

We are all susceptible to human failings. We've all pointed the finger of blame at ourselves and others and trotted out an inner perfectionist to bludgeon ourselves with guilt and shame. We have crushed the delicate violet of another's feelings and trampled our own under the heels of unrealistic demands. But as the imminently true cliche states, "To err is human, to forgive, divine." As we forgive, the divine fragrance of the Beloved flows through us, bestowing blessings.

Our souls are no strangers to forgiveness, for they have basked in the benediction of God's forgiveness for eternity. Difficulty in forgiving means that we have slipped from the heart of God into our human heads or guts and are no longer centered in the ground of our being, which is unconditional love.

By becoming aware of the skid away from our higher self, we can move back into our hearts. Even though it may sound too good to be true, we *can* return to our heart by merely asking to do so and accepting that it is done. Remembering to pour the fragrance of God's love and acceptance upon ourselves will set the stage for our ability to forgive the hands that occasionally crush us.

Forgiving ourselves allows us to create a garden of violets that will perfume our own and other's lives with the fragrance of love.

I am willing to forgive myself.

I forgive myself.

Extending Forgiveness

FORGIVENESS IS NOT OPTIONAL IF YOU WISH TO walk a spiritual path. Practicing the art of forgiveness is essential for keeping our spirits green and gloriously alive. Not being able or willing to forgive those who have hurt us blocks God's love from entering our hearts and dams the flow of love going from us toward others.

Not forgiving binds us to our tormentor and to the original injury, keeping it fresh and current even if it is actually old and stale. Definitely a losing proposition! In reality, we don't forgive someone because it is good for the other person; we forgive in order to free our own hearts and souls and return ourselves to a state of love.

Tiffany was finding it very difficult to forgive her mother, who drank herself to death when Tiffany was a teenager. The years preceding her mother's death were filled with neglect and embarrassment that had left deep scars. Grieving the fact that she had never really had a mother and venting her anger about her loss was important in Tiffany's healing. But eventually she realized that she didn't want to carry the ghost of her mother on her back for the rest of her life, and so she made a commitment to forgiving her.

Tiffany found it very helpful to picture her

mother and then imagine that she could look *through* the drinker's facade and see the wounded, scared, and ignorant part of her mother who needed to disrupt everyone's lives. It was much easier to forgive the little girl inside her mother, who had also had a difficult childhood, than it was to forgive the woman who had made Tiffany's miserable.

In any forgiveness practice, it's important to remember that we can't see the whole spiritual picture. We don't know precisely what lessons our souls have signed up for in their evolutionary process. What we do know is that being able to forgive ourselves and others opens our hearts to the flow of divine energy.

I am willing to forgive _____.

I forgive _____.

Exploring the Family Tree

IF WE HAVE ARID PLACES IN US FROM OUR
experience with our parents, a great way to re-
green them is to learn to understand, honor, and
know our parents as human beings, not roles. If
they are alive, we can talk to them about their
childhoods and, by listening to their reminiscences,
get a better feel for why and how they became the
people they are. If our parents have died, we can
talk to other family members and friends about
them and explore letters and papers left behind.

Out of a deep desire to know who her father
really was, Carrie created a four-page questionnaire
and sent it to him. It had easy questions like, "What
is your favorite color?" and "What were your parents like?" and tough ones such as, "How did you
want me to think or feel about my sexuality?" and
"Do you think about your own death, and are you
afraid?" Although it took him a while to respond,
to his credit, this quiet man attempted to answer
most of his daughter's questions.

Carrie told me that his answers gave her a feeling of comfort and calm, an increased sense of why
she is who she is, and a richer picture of her background. She better understands the influences that
shaped both herself and her father, and she feels
closer to him as a result.

In knowing our parents, we can more fully know ourselves. Ask yourself how you might be able to know your parents more authentically and decide what actions you want to take that are appropriate to your circumstances. Doing so may feel like a risk, but, who knows—within their histories, you may find an oasis for yourself.

Our personalities yearn to know and understand our souls. And when either is revealed, the other becomes more transparent, more readily available.

I love to learn about my background.

I love and honor myself and my parents.

Trailing Clouds of Glory

GENE AND I RECENTLY BECAME GRANDPARENTS for the first time, and I am learning that nothing re-greens the heart and mind quite like being in the presence of an innocent infant. William Wordsworth was certainly right in his poem *Ode on Immortality* when he said, "But trailing clouds of glory do we come from God, who is our home: Heaven lies about us in our infancy!"

I've always gone to pet stores or stopped people on the street with infants, puppies, or kittens to get my baby-fixes, but the other day I stepped back just a little to view other family members reacting to my little grandbaby's first smiles. We had all turned into "people-puddles," melting in the warmth of the absolutely pure energy he embodies and showers on us. It's a two-way street—he opens our hearts with the aura of Heaven he trails, and we enfold him in love and security.

Not only can we make sure that we get a baby-fix every now and then, but we can re-green arid places within us by giving to and gleaning from our own inner little ones.

Pam's mother died only a few days after she was born and Pam was cared for by a well-meaning but unprepared aunt who, not unnaturally, was a bit resentful at the unexpected turn of events in her life. As an adult, Pam avoided intimate relationships, rationalizing that she was too busy with her career. In truth, being a motherless daughter had left her carrying the unconscious belief that she was unlovable.

Finally, chronic depression made her seek therapy, where she discovered she needed to become the mother to herself that she'd never had. Through guided meditation, journaling, and a dogged determination to feel better, Pam began to love her inner infant and ultimately came to twin realizations: that she was not responsible for her mother's death and that she was infinitely lovable.

If you're feeling somewhat barren or lifeless, treat yourself to a baby-fix—either inner or outer—and immerse yourself in the innocent Heaven of new life.

I allow new life of all kinds to renew me.

I love my own inner little one.

Accepting Love from the Beloved

. . . .

ONE OF THE BEST WAYS TO RE-GREEN ARID places in our psyches is to cultivate the skill of accepting and absorbing love What is more nurturing than resting in the tender embrace of a loved one? What revitalizes us as much as feeling gently and unconditionally accepted? Very little, and yet it is often hard for us to both accept love and to ask for it. As with any skill, however, we can learn how to do it.

Gayle, a client of mine, was going through a very painful divorce. As a result, she felt betrayed, enraged, terrified, and totally unlovable. Although her friends and family tried to love and support her, she found it almost impossible to accept what they, or I, offered. As we worked together and her anger and terror dissipated somewhat, Gayle realized that the "plexiglass dome" she'd erected around herself was only serving to alienate her kids and make everyone, including herself, increasingly miserable. In a wonderfully passionate manner, Gayle decided that the best way to "get even with the bad guy" was to be happy.

Knowing that the ability to accept love was a big step toward happiness, Gayle committed herself to mastering the skill. She began each morning by telling her reflection in the mirror, "I love you" or, on really hard days, "I'm, sort of, a little willing to love you." A very determined woman, each day Gayle visualized herself being in the presence of a loving and caring spiritual being, and she practiced consciously accepting love from her. At first the exercise was very hard and felt phony, but she persevered. Next she practiced laying her hands on her heart and asking it to open when her children offered her love or she wanted to show love to them.

Although it took quite a while for Gayle to heal her hurt and learn to once more embrace love, today she is a happy woman with a close relationship to God, herself, and her family.

You, too, can become adept at welcoming love. Make a commitment today to be open to accepting love, and visualize being held in a loving embrace by the Great Spirit.

God is the Beloved who kisses me on the inside of my heart.

I am worthy of love.

Balancing God's Qualities

. . . .

I'VE HEARD IT SAID THAT IF GOD IS MALE, then the male is God, and in our predominately patriarchal culture, God's masculinity does remain the prevalent belief system. But in this belief something crucial to us all has been left out—the Feminine. Indeed the loss of the Feminine from our spiritual ideologies has caused a grief so deep and so raw, particularly in women, that it has been virtually unspeakable until recently. Why? Because, as women, we have been disinherited; we are not created in His image. In her book, *A God Who Looks Like Me*, Patricia Reilly beautifully addresses the wounding some women feel around this issue.

But the loss is not women's alone. No matter how we may feel about the idea of a purely male God, it is obvious that when the Divine is only masculine, only male qualities are highly valued. This leaves the feminine qualities of compassion, inclusion, cooperation, tolerance, beingness, intuition, and nurturance underrated and even perceived as weak or ineffective. With the negation of heart-qualities such as these comes many of the malignancies in society; lack of empathy, elevation of power, violence, disregard for nature, concentration solely on the mind to the exclusion of the heart, and loss of soul, to name only a few.

In a human family, it is optimal when both loving masculine and feminine models are available. The same is true within our spiritual family. Believing in and honoring both the masculine and feminine divinity within our hearts, and within the great unknowable mystery that is God, is essential for the balance and harmony of our spirits.

We need both the law and the love, the word and the wisdom, the mind and the heart of God. With tender honesty, ask yourself if the God that you love possesses both feminine and masculine aspects. If not, make a commitment to give yourself a sacred gift by incorporating the missing virtues into your heart's vision of the Beloved.

I honor and appreciate both the masculine and the feminine qualities of the Divine.

I possess qualities worthy of honor and admiration.

Finding the Motherhood of God

ALTHOUGH I BELIEVE THAT GOD IS BIGGER THAN I can ever hope to fathom and embodies both masculine and feminine qualities, I often feel a deep yearning to sit at the feet of an ideal Mother God to be consoled or taught.

It wasn't until my own mother's last illness that I became fully aware of how much I longed for an unconditionally loving female presence. I wanted, both within me and in my spiritual ideology, a guide and plumb line who represented the feminine principles of love, wisdom, and patience. Jolted by the recognition that my most important female influence would soon be unavailable in physical form, I began to pray for and meditate on a feminine aspect of God to whom I could relate.

God responded to my request in beautiful ways. Teachers appeared as I was ready, and the two most important things I learned from them were very simple: *Your desire is valid and essential* and *Trust your images.*

As I began to trust my own images, they became clearer and more frequent. Right now, I'm aware of several female beings who comfort and guide me. One in particular, whom I call "The Lady," appeared as a result of a knocked-to-my-knees, end-of-my-rope plea. She is incredibly strong, about seven feet tall, infinitely wise, and impersonally compassionate.

Please understand that I realize that I haven't a clue as to the reality of the mystery of God. The best I can do is love, honor, and serve the images that resonate with my heart at this time. But frankly, I don't think God cares what we call Him/Her/All, as long as we keep in touch.

I trust my images of God.

I ask for the Mother God who is right for me.

Walking the Earth with Sensitive Feet

. . . .

IN A PERPETUAL DANCE, EARTH AND SKY provide us with a beautiful life-sustaining environment. Just when Mother Earth pulls back into her roots to replenish and revitalize, leaving her queendom brown and barren, Father Sky fills his realm with a carnival of clouds that bring moisture to a parched planet. Working in concert, they never leave us with a time when our eyes cannot be dazzled, our hearts uplifted in awe, and our lungs filled with air. Regretfully, ignorance and greed are damaging both earth and sky as we humans act as if there is an extra earth in the attic.

One outcome of living more in harmony with the Spirit will be a natural increase in awareness about the need to care for our planet. It is the literal ground of our being, and both Mother Earth and Father Sky need us to be sensitive to what harms them. We are planetary stewards and must learn to treat our home with respect and care.

Every now and then I travel to sacred spots with a group of spiritually-minded women. Recently we went to Arches National Park in Moab, Utah, where Mother Nature has responded to the elements of wind and water by creating breathtaking sculptures, awesome in size and beauty. One of the goals of these excursions is to consciously bless the earth and restore energy to places that may have been depleted through misuse.

On this trip, we spent two hours silently in the presence of the incredible arches. The single suggestion made by one of the leaders before we began was to hold the sentiment, "I see you from afar, and I am longing for your healing" as we experienced Mother Earth. Afterward, one woman's comment especially struck me: "I promised that I will walk the earth with sensitive feet."

How different our world would be if we all walked everywhere with sensitive feet! Take a moment today to consider your relationship with nature. How can you walk the earth with more sensitive feet?

I appreciate and care for the planet.

I see you from afar, and I am longing for your healing.

Learning from the Stones

GLEANING WISDOM FROM INDIGENOUS AND Eastern cultures that revere their elders, our heretofore youth-worshiping society is finally learning to let go of "age anxiety" and value the patina that aging can bring to the soul. Of course not all people magically become wise and wonderful as they age, but those who choose to look at what they gain from advancing years, rather than what they lose, generally have a lustrous heart and a gleam in their eyes.

Ideally, the experiences accrued throughout the years bring increased wisdom and instill an inner security that allows us to speak our truth fearlessly and act from an unshakable sense of integrity. I love the quote from Dorothy Sayers: "Time and trouble will tame an advanced young woman, but an advanced old woman is uncontrollable by any earthly force." Yes. For the good of the whole, we need to be uncontrollable and untamed in our efforts to invite the spirit of love to quench the thirst of our souls and re-green our world.

I saw the beauty of aging exemplified by nature while on my trip to Arches National Park. In silent meditation, I sat in the protective shade of an eons-old rock that I came to think of as "Grandmother Rock." Gazing through the unbelievably huge arch in her facing sister, I was awed by the beauty created as this stone adapted to the elements and, over the millennium, grew a window through which the pristine sky gleams.

In the face of her patient transformation from one kind of beauty to another, I found myself asking how I was being called to mature as I age. What sandy sediment within me needs to erode away? What window into my very soul is yearning to be revealed in my walled-in personal world? What must be transformed in me in order for my transparency to reveal a vast and changing sky? I have no answers, only the knowledge that they will come if I remain open to the questions.

I am thankful for the wisdom, experience, and acceptance gleaned through aging.

I am an outrageous and untamed champion of love and learning.

Filling the Well

A DRY WELL IRRIGATES NOTHING. IF WE ARE TO be gloriously and outrageously alive, as Hildegaard of Bingen encourages us at the beginning of this section, we need to fill our inner wells regularly.

I love the metaphor, "God is an underground river, ever present and constantly flowing within and around us." But, even if we believe in an eternal river, do we take the time to fill our wells from it, or do we allow them to go dry?

Although the source is the same, the ways in which we fill our wells are unique and individual. What fills your well of spirit? What fills your well of emotion and physical well-being?

Close your eyes for a moment and allow a picture of a well to come into your mind's eye. Without judgment, explore your well. Is it full? How do you feel about it? What, if anything, does it need from you? Cleaning? Rebuilding? Take a few minutes to recreate it in a way that appeals to you. Perhaps you want your well to be the focal point of a beautiful garden or to stand in the midst of a clearing of majestic redwoods. Trust the images that your wise subconscious presents.

When your well pleases you, allow it to open to receive the pure waters of the eternal underground river of God. At the same time, begin to fill it from

OUR HEARTS ARE POWERFUL SAGES which embody the wisdom, intuition, and compassion of the ages. They *know*, on a soul level, what is loving and nurturing, and they also deeply understand what connects us to the Divine. Given the chance, our hearts have the ability not only to help us become more loving but also to find fulfillment, peace of mind, increased creativity, and optimum health.

Intuitively, both the enlightened and the ordinary among us have known that love's transformative power can actually conquer all, and we believe that our hearts speak a different, more caring language than do our minds. But being believers doesn't automatically make us doers. Activating the power of our hearts takes practice and consistent intention, but we can tap into the mysterious energy of love for which our spirits thirst.

Realizing God's Love

. . . .

IT GIVES ME GREAT COMFORT TO BELIEVE THAT
there never was, and never will be, a time when my
essence was not beloved by God. As the wonderful
mystic, Julian of Norwich, suggested when she
said, "Between God and the soul, there is no
between," I've come to realize that the distance I
can feel between myself and God is not created by
Her but by me. She is ever present, the pure ema-
nation of heart-energy, attempting to love me into
the awareness that I, too, am, in essence, heart-
energy.

One of our most important spiritual tasks is to
come to the realization of God's unending and
unconditional love. The security of knowing that
God loves us is the cornerstone of our soul-growth.
As Anne Morrow Lindbergh said, "The most
exhausting thing in life . . . is being insecure." Insecurity *is* exhausting, because it's riddled with fear
and, therefore, barricades us from our hearts. Fear
and love cannot coexist, and so, when we are in a
state of fear, we cannot access the love that surrounds us constantly.

For many of us, this love is hard to experience.
To give you a sense of security with God, the
Beloved, allow yourself to close your eyes and
imagine that you are in a beautiful place where you

feel comfortable and accepted. Rest in the peace of your place. Begin to breathe deeply, in through your nose and out through your mouth. With each inhalation, draw into your heart a feeling of well-being, and as you exhale give yourself permission to breathe out any feelings of stress or uneasiness.

As you become more relaxed, notice that you are holding in your arms someone whom you genuinely love. It may be a baby or child, a pet, or a loved one. Breathe into your heart and allow love to flow from it to the other person's heart. After a few minutes, very gently change places and feel yourself being held in the lap of a benevolent presence who loves you deeply and unconditionally. If this is difficult for you, without judgment, become the holder again and pour love from your heart onto the person being held. Feel the outpouring of love surround you as it enfolds them. Slowly allow the picture to alter and imagine yourself feeling loved as you nestle in the welcoming lap of God.

Before the beginning God loved me.

God is loving me now.

Cleansing Our Hearts

. . . .

OUR HEARTS NOT ONLY ENCOMPASS THE
strongest and wisest aspects of our nature, but also
the softest and most vulnerable ones as well.
Because life can be difficult, our hearts may become
encrusted with feelings of fear and disillusionment
or stained by sorrow and self-deprecating beliefs.
Even if our lives have been utterly smooth, without
a single pebble upon our path, we may have at least
gathered a little dust along the way.

Because Spirit moves more freely through a
clear heart, we can best embody heart energy when
we cleanse our hearts. Doing so will provide an
unobstructed passage through which God's love
can flow.

When you can find a few quiet moments—even
if it is before falling asleep tonight or arising tomorrow morning—tenderly perform a heart check.
With your eyes closed, place your hands over your
heart and tell it that you love it. Sincerely thank
your heart for its absolute faithfulness. Now see or
sense the condition of your heart. Trust your wise
intuition; whatever appears is probably the perfect
symbol for you right now. Does it look clean? Does
it feel clear? If not, ask what you can do right now
to cleanse and heal your heart. Honor the answer,
even if it seems strange.

The last time I meditated on this, my heart was a little sad and had a small bruise at the tip. It was appreciative of my caring and wanted to be bathed in warm sea water and then have a poultice of lotus leaves applied to the bruise.

In the theater of my mind, I went to a favorite Hawaiian beach where the surf is gentle and soothing. Effortlessly floating in the warm, tropical water, I imagined it flowing through me, gently caressing and buoying up my heart. As a lotus drifted toward me, I held its pink leaves to my chest and asked that they heal the bruised area and cleanse my heart.

I cleanse and clear my heart when it needs it.

I invite the Spirit to flow easily through my heart.

Opening Our Hearts

. . . .

LOVE IS NOT MEANT TO BE HELD IN A CLENCHED heart. Like water, love must be allowed to flow naturally and freely or it becomes grabby and turns into attachment and dependence. Fear is usually the icy fist that seizes our heart, clanging it closed. When our heart is locked behind iron doors, we're cut off from its innate wisdom and compassion, both of which are necessary for us to feel truly happy and fulfilled.

For our heart to be willing and able to open, we must dispel its fear and protect it from harm. Although no one can really wound our heart unless we allow it, fear keeps us from realizing that fact. As a wily adversary, fear is most easily transformed by the light of creative visualization.

Some of the visualizations that I and my clients use to allay fears include: seeing and feeling the hands of Christ over our hearts brushing away danger; putting on a magic, impermeable cloak; surrounding our hearts in an orb of white light; placing an invisible filter between ourselves and another; and being shielded by an angel.

It doesn't matter what you choose, only that it works for you. One whimsical client of mine imagines herself riding a huge white unicorn into tricky situations. If a barb or fear flies her way, her unicorn snags it on his magical horn and flings it harmlessly away. She knows that humor and fun help disperse fear.

Design a visualization that makes you feel safe and secure and relax into it. As you enjoy your personal mind-movie, begin to breathe more and more deeply. Invite any heart-closing fears to parade by and watch as your protectors render them impotent. Still surrounded by protection, visualize your heart opening in its perfect, right time and way. As it opens, feel the security and well-being flowing into it as you inhale, and feel that same sense of well-being flowing out to the world as you exhale. In and out. Gently, lovingly, and safely.

I protect my heart.

From my open heart flows pure love.

Cradling a Wounded Heart

DURING AN EXTREMELY PAINFUL TIME IN MY LIFE, I vowed to never be hurt that badly again. To protect myself, I armored my heart so effectively that it felt as if it began to atrophy from lack of use. Only with my children did I feel safe enough to give and receive love. Thank goodness—for without those kids, my soul might have withered and wafted away.

Luckily, my spirit began to rebel against its ever-increasing grayness and encouraged me to choose love rather than reclusive safety. At first I refused and huddled resolutely behind my armor. There must have been some spark of willingness within me for, as Spirit persisted, caring and helpful people began to appear in my life.

Annabelle, a wonderful woman who would become my spiritual mother, was an important guide. Knowing that I had an advocate whom I could call if I were desperate gave me the courage to creep around the corner of my armor and begin to heal my heart. The transformation process was neither fast nor easy but began to happen as soon as I started cradling my wounded heart.

As you would to an injured child, I crooned to my heart that everything would be okay, that I would protect and nurture it, that I would keep it as safe as possible. When I was too weak to be nurturing, I visualized my mother, Annabelle, an angel, or Mary, Christ's mother, holding the wounded part of me in soothing, comforting arms and infusing my heart with healing energy. During times when I was too bottomed-out to do anything myself, I called a friend and asked her to hold me in her prayers.

If your heart is wounded, console and comfort it, and don't hesitate to reach out to others for help in doing so.

I hold my heart in the gentle arms of love.

I allow others to help me heal.

Growing a Grinch Heart

HEART-CENTERED THINKERS KNOW INTUITIVELY that love is power. As Anne Morrow Lindbergh wrote, "Love is a force . . . it is not a result; it is a cause. It is not a product; it produces. It is a power, like money, or steam, or electricity. It is valueless unless you can give something else by means of it."

As mentioned in the introduction, science is now underscoring our intuitive awareness with measurable data. One Institute of HeartMath study that appealed to me shows that our hearts are the strongest amplifying system we have for generating positive electrical fields. When subjects in the laboratory brought their attention to their hearts and augmented that attention with feelings of appreciation and caring, computer printouts displayed greatly increased fields of energy emanating from their hearts in ever-widening circles.

The picture HeartMath has drawn of this phenomenon reminded me of Dr. Seuss' story of *The Grinch Who Stole Christmas*. The Grinch's heart was finally touched by the Whos in Whoville, when they still exhibited the spirit of Christmas even after all of their gifts and decorations had been stolen. Feeling what I guess was amazement and appreciation for the Whos, the Grinch's heart grew from a tiny dried up tidbit into a radiantly beautiful starburst filling his entire chest. Rays of heart-energy poured from him toward the little Whos happily singing below.

All of us can grow a Grinch heart. Quietly close your eyes and focus your attention on your heart area. Bring into your awareness a sense of deep appreciation for a person or situation. Bask in the resultant feelings and allow your heart to expand. See and feel your heart-energy amplified and enlarged, blessing you first, and then moving out to grace others with the gift of love.

Love is truly a force for good, and we can amplify our output.

My heart is continuously growing.

I give love graciously.

Roaming in the Heart

SO OFTEN WE ALLOW OUR MINDS TO ROAM IN areas that are not conducive to feeling good. We ramble around in the past in hopes of a better yesterday, and then we leap ahead and scurry fretfully around in the "what ifs" of the future. As a consequence, most of us spend very little time in the present moment, tuned into what is going on right now.

One particularly destructive mind habit—one of my own major weaknesses—is to rehash and relive negative emotional experiences, gnawing them, and our nerves, to shreds. Not good, because five minutes of ruminating on an argument creates the same imbalance in the autonomic nervous system as does real-time anger, and it depletes the immune system for several hours afterward. Roaming in emotional minefields is bad for our physical, emotional, and spiritual health.

Diametrically opposed to the effects we get from straying into negativity are the positive effects received by roaming in the fields of our heart, the "hub of all sacred places" according to Sri Nityananda. Here we learn to be present to what is, right now, without being mired in the past or grasping for the future. Find a quiet moment today and allow your body to settle into a comfortable position. Encourage your body to soften, your breath to deepen, and your mind to be still. Focus on your breath and watch as it automatically begins to slow down. Bring your attention to your heart. Feel gratitude and admiration for it.

As you relax, create a beautiful scene that is symbolic of your heart. If the picture that first appears doesn't appeal to you, let it fade and create a new one. Explore your heartscape; deeply enjoy and appreciate what it generously offers. Be open to surprise blessings that may arise. You can invite those whom you love to join you, or you may prefer to have a solitary experience. Whatever you choose, trust the intuition of your heart to provide a scene that is right for you now.

During the day, refresh yourself by taking minute vacations to come into the present moment. Return to the sacred hub of your heart and roam in it.

My heart is sacred.

I am worthy of a heartscape that is beautiful and refreshing.

Soothing Our Hearts

BECAUSE WE KNOW BEST WHEN OUR SPIRITS have been mowed down by a Mac truck, or merely nicked by a moped, it's up to us to soothe our hearts and souls and be willing to ask for soothing from others.

While out on the road promoting *Heart Centered Marriage*, my heart gave me ample evidence that it needed some lovin' care. It was one of those days that you'd like to erase from the calendar, culminating with a talk I gave at a large bookstore. Six people showed up; one was a heckler and two (including my own escort) fell asleep, and, even worse, only two books were sold at the end of my presentation. My heart felt as if it were petrifying inside my chest and I could scarcely breathe. By the time I limped back to my hotel, I was the lowest of the low.

I called my husband and a friend for support and neither were home. "See, you're not even important to *them!*" wailed a vulnerable inner voice before a wiser, more mature, message could make itself heard and said, "Looks like you're on your own for this one, Toots. Practice what you preach."

First, as if it were a cherished baby, I held my book over my heart and told it that it was very, very good. You can do this with any creation or idea of yours. Our creations carry an energy that links with our own. As we reassure them, we reassure ourselves. Then I did the following exercise. If you've had a recent disappointment, or felt badly about yourself for some reason, you too might benefit from it.

With your hands over your heart, pour love into your heart and to the part of you that feels inadequate or upset. Gently soothe your heart with consoling affirmations such as, "I love you. I honor you. You are a wonderful and loving heart. I value you. I take care of you. I listen to you, and I will protect you."

We all have vulnerable aspects of our being that need to be soothed on occasion. It is our sacred charge to comfort our hurting hearts.

I compassionately soothe my aching heart.
I love and comfort my vulnerable selves.

Surrendering Head to Heart

. . . .

FOR CENTURIES THE HEAD HAS RULED THE roost. "I think therefore I am" has been the credo of our left-brain-dominated society, and, as a consequence, the whole world is out of balance. Individually and universally, we need to return to the balance and harmony that can be achieved only by training our heads to surrender to the wisdom and compassion of our hearts.

When I broached this subject to Martha, a client of mine who is a very business-oriented realtor, she paled and said, "Sue, you can't be serious! If I follow my heart I won't be able to survive in this competitive, dog-eat-dog field." I told her that I didn't think her fears would materialize and, skeptically, she agreed to do the following meditation for about three minutes each morning until I saw her again in two weeks.

At her next appointment, Martha's fears were somewhat quieted. She told me, "Well, I didn't *lose* any business, but I didn't *gain* any either! I have noticed a funny thing. I feel less stressed and my clients seem to have gotten nicer." My bet is that Martha, herself, is sending out a calmer heart frequency that makes her clients feel more comfortable around her. That's not only good for her, but it's also good for business.

You too can benefit from the balance between heart and head. With your eyes closed, breathe deeply into your heart area and feel it accepting and absorbing the life-giving infusion. Imagine that your heart is expanding and that loving energy is flowing from its center like circles on the surface of a pond. With reverence, physically bow your head toward your heart. Even if it feels awkward, silently tell your heart that your head wishes to cooperate with it, surrender to it, and serve it. Ask your heart's inherent wisdom and love to guide you.

My head surrenders to my heart.

My heart is a wise and compassionate guide.

Softening in the Face of Hardness

CAMILLA HAD MADE A PROMISE TO HERSELF that, as a part of her spiritual discipline, she would learn to soften her responses, attitudes, and judgments. Because she was prone to feeling defensive when faced with difficult situations or people, she decided to use such events as reminders to soften. Right off the bat, her husband (our mates are always such good teachers) provided her with the perfect opportunity when he surprisingly overreacted to a suggestion she made.

Feeling as if she'd been kicked in the stomach, Camilla nonetheless remembered that here was an opportunity to soften. Although she managed to keep her response quiet, her judgments where flaring inside and her heart felt hard and constricted. She excused herself and went to a private place where she attempted to tune into her heart. Quieting her mind was like wrestling with a two year old in the midst of a temper tantrum, but finally she was able to get in touch with her heart. First she comforted and forgave the person within her who felt hurt, frustrated, and angry. When she was calmer, she asked her heart what to do in this situation. The answer was an unequivocal, "Relax and back off."

Relaxing and backing off while there was a rift

between herself and her husband was not exactly Camilla's first choice or best talent, but she did as her heart suggested. Later that evening, her patience was rewarded when her husband told her that he had had a troublesome business reversal right before their flare-up. Intuitively she realized that this was his way of explaining his reaction and that an escalation of bad feelings between them had been avoided by her backing off.

Although it's often difficult to do, softening in the face of hardness allows us to return to our hearts where true strength and peace of mind reside.

I can be safe and soft at the same time.

Faced with hardness, I remember to soften.

Weaving Essence and Experience

. . . .

OUR ESSENCE IS SPIRIT, AND OUR EXPERIENCE IS human. Therefore, while our essence is always love, our experiences can be ragged, flawed, or downright icky. The trick is to infuse experience with essence and weave them together, for it is through our very humanness in conjunction with Spirit that our soul grows. We need not subjugate nor negate our humanness in order to become a vessel of love, but rather become the best human we can be. Through love and acceptance, we can transform our human limitations into a clear window through which our essence can shine. Healing, honing, and honoring our humanity encourages us to become the best possible vehicle for the light of Spirit.

Because her husband is a football fan and she likes to participate in activities with him, Sylvia has learned to transform the experience of going to a football game into a spiritual opportunity. Silently fuming about what a stupid and dangerous sport football was used to ruin the outings for Sylvia, but now she sends love and protective light to all of the players. In weaving her essence into football experiences, she is also creating a stronger bond with her husband.

Play with the concept of weaving for a minute. Close your eyes and relax and, in whatever way feels right to you, give yourself permission to create a fanciful tapestry of your life. Imagine a color or colors for both your essence and your experience. You can choose one particular experience or focus on experiences in general. Anything is perfectly alright.

Ask both the wisdom and the whimsy of your heart to help weave the colors of essence and experience together in a symbolic picture. What do you love about the weaving? What do you dislike, or what makes you uncomfortable?

Study your tapestry as you would a dream. There are undoubtedly valuable hints in this meditation about how you feel you're doing with the task of weaving essence and experience together. As we become more adept at bringing our essence into everyday experiences, they will be magically transformed into everyday blessings.

I accept and honor both my essence and my experiences.

Bathed in love, all experiences can become blessings.

Lightening Up

. . . .

HUMOR IS A WONDERFUL HEART ENERGY, A proven leavening agent. Without humor, our lives become increasingly colorless and drab. Yet in our hectic daily schedules, it's easy to let obligation and frustration drain our humor veins, leaving us with a pallor becoming only to an android or a vampire.

One of the best ways to invite humor back into our lives and spark up our spirits is to be in the presence of children and to really pay attention to them. If little ones aren't available to you, see if you can find a playmate in the child within yourself and encourage her to help you lighten up.

Janie, a dear friend of mine, was inching along in traffic, totally frustrated. Every now and then she'd hit the steering wheel muttering something akin to, "Come *on!!!*" Finally, from the backseat, her beautiful, angelic-looking two-year-old daughter piped up with a suggestion, "Say fuggum, Mommy!" Nonplussed, but thoroughly amused, Janie felt her spirits immediately lift. Delight and appreciation for her daughter's unintended wit opened her heart, causing traffic to take a backseat to love and laughter. For years, Janie and I would say, "Just say *fuggum*, Mommy!" to each other when we were crabby.

As Art Linkletter well knew, kids say the darndest things, and those wee wisdoms often help us laugh ourselves to lightness. We always have our internal kid-comedian with us, and it will help us immeasurably if we can encourage her to feel free to say the darndest things to us. The car is a great place to practice for two reasons; traffic *is* frustrating, and no one can hear our silliness.

This may seem frivolous to you, but it really isn't. Any means we can employ to embody more heart energy and lighten up our lives are good. Young children and healed inner children are natural sources of heartful—not hurtful—humor. Take some time today to do something impractical and fun.

I laugh easily and naturally.

I encourage my inner kid to come out and play.

Bearing Beams of Love

. . . .

WE ARE HERE TO DO GOOD. TO LIVE OUT OUR spiritual purpose, we are called to appreciate, honor, empower, and listen to ourselves and to others who speak to us: To be the good we are meant to be. Poet William Blake stated this sentiment beautifully when he wrote, "We are here but for a little while to learn to bear the beams of love."

Beams of love originate in and emanate from our hearts. Our hearts are individual, internal wisdom teachers consistently nudging us toward a higher degree of consciousness and more ability to love.

Ancient sages reside within our hearts bearing torches from which the beams of love flow. They welcome our calls for counsel and guidance.

It often helps to have a visual reference on which to draw when thinking about our heart teachers. Toward that end, please close your eyes and use any technique that works for you to move into a restful state of mind. In your mind's eye, see yourself seated at a beautiful campfire in the gathering dusk. Ask your heart to provide you with a picture or sense of the teacher, or teachers, who reside within in it. Invite them to share the light of your fire. If you don't feel loved by and safe with the ones who come, erase them and repeat the invitation. When the appropriate teachers appear, bask in their presence. Present them with any questions that come to your mind. Listen carefully. Answers may be heard, sensed intuitively, or seen as symbols. At the end of your time together, ask your teachers how best to communicate with them in the future. Thank them for appearing.

I listen to the wisdom of my heart's sages.
I send forth beams of light and love.

Being Truly Nice

I RECENTLY MET JILL, A YOUNG WOMAN WHO IS a joy to be around. Everyone loves her and gravitates toward her. I can see why, because she is genuinely nice to each person she encounters. Recently I watched her interact with Priscilla, her difficult-to-get-along-with mother-in-law.

While Priscilla was grumping about something—a fairly consistent habit of hers—Jill silently reached over and stroked her arm. No judgment, just an accepting presence. During the entire weekend I was in her company, I never heard Jill say anything that wasn't upbeat. Consequently, we all felt good around her—safe, seen, even savored.

Niceness sometimes connotes wimpiness, but that interpretation usually comes from the fact that many of us have felt that it was expected of us to *make* nice even when we didn't *feel* nice. When we realize that niceness is a natural outgrowth of deep kindness and caring, we can consciously choose to develop our niceness quotient. We can set our intention to truly *being* nice, rather than putting on a phony nice front. Often, the simple desire to grow our soul through niceness helps us focus on coming from our hearts where true niceness flourishes.

It's perfectly okay to act nice even when we

don't feel it as long as we're doing so from personal choice, not from a sense of obligation or fear. Freely choosing to act nice will actually help us begin to embody the authentic niceness of our hearts.

Nice not only *wears* well, but, generally, it also *fares* well, for kindness is never out-of-date or out-of-style and is welcome in all circles. Everyone enjoys being uplifted in the safe haven of nice attitudes and actions. Being truly nice, as Jill is, makes us a heart-lifter.

I choose to act in kind and caring ways.

I am a heart-lifter.

Inviting Intuition In

INTUITION IS KNOWING WHAT WE KNOW WITH-out knowing how we know it. Because intuition is perceiving and understanding without conscious reasoning, it's a shortcut to learning for us. It works so fast that our minds need time to figure out what our intuitive hearts know immediately.

Because we live in a society that is so focused on the knowledge that comes from our heads, our task as we seek a stronger connection to Spirit is to have the courage to trust the intuitive voice that whispers to us. As we learn to trust our intuition and invite it more fully into our awareness, it will breathe a sigh of relief and say, "Ah, good. I've been waiting here in your heart to be recognized and relied on."

The beauty of intuition is that it is smarter than any problem and comes from a much higher source than does opinion. Intuition is more grounded in ancient wisdom and its input comes from realms other than the conscious. Opinion is colored by many brushes, but intuition comes from the heart and is untainted by outside influence.

Just a year ago, my husband Gene's intuition saved me untold heartache. He was scheduled to leave the house early one morning and be gone most of the day on errands, but he felt uneasy about leaving and stalled his departure. Hesitation is exceedingly unusual for him, but it soon became clear that his intuition was warning him that he would be needed at home. Right before he was about to force himself out the door, my sister called to say that my father had had a heart attack. Because Gene was home and is great at logistics and arranging travel, I was able to make it to Dad's side in time to have a meaningful "I love you, goodbye" conversation before he died. Thank God that Gene invited his intuition into his awareness! My heart is so much better off because he listened to his.

You, too, regularly receive nudges from your heart. By listening, you invite the wisdom of intuition into your life.

I listen to my heart's whispers.
My intuition is wise and trustworthy.

Freeing the Spirit of Peace and Love

*Peace and love are alive in us, but we are not
always alive in peace and love.*

—Julian of Norwich

RETURNING TO OUR HEARTS IS SUCH A SIMPLE
concept that we may feel tempted to downplay its
significance but we mustn't, because a conscious
return to our hearts frees the spirit of love and
peace within us. And each of us—as well as the
world as a whole—is thirsting for the solace of living within the safety and serenity of love and peace.

When our hearts are ignored, they become
crusted over, which naturally cuts peace and love
out of our day-to-day life. Within a neglected
heart, the spirit of love is imprisoned, unable to
share its healing energy with us or all the others
who need it. By returning to our hearts, we reclaim
the Sacred Feminine Voice whose values include
not only peace and love but also tolerance, acceptance, compassion, intuitive wisdom, cooperation,
and complementation. Reinstating these heart-centered values will not only enliven us but will also
reap rich rewards for our children and our planet.

Gently close your eyes and pay attention to
your heart area. In a few moments, begin to visualize a door behind which you will find your heart.

Carefully, but without judgment, notice what the door looks like. If it is barricaded or blocked, ask for help from your guardian angel, or any wise guide that you relate to, to open it. Once inside, imagine that you are met by a radiantly strong and compassionate feminine being. In her hands she holds symbols for both peace and love. Question her about how you can bring these qualities alive within your life.

At the end of this meditation, it might be a good idea to make a note of the ideas you received from the Sacred Feminine Voice within your heart and post it as a reminder. Choosing to bring peace and love alive within ourselves by coming from our hearts on a consistent basis is the hope of the world.

The spirit of peace and love is strong and free within me.

I listen to my Sacred Feminine Voice.

Siphoning Off Stress

. . . .

ONE OF THE WAYS WE TEND TO SLIP FROM OUR loving hearts into our reactive guts is to become overwhelmed by stress. A little stress is necessary to create some get-up-and-go, but too much can overpower us and short out our circuits. Stress is the four-letter word of our time. Who hasn't felt stressed out, tension-ridden, and temper-tattered at one time or another? How can we siphon off the excess stress that blocks our ability to live from our hearts?

There are many short-term stress-busters such as drinking, overeating, and being bitchy that we want to avoid because they are unhealthy and create shame and strained relationships. Healthily siphoning off excess stress is a three-fold process.

First, we need to become mentally aware of the stress and let it go before it reaches red-alert status. Second, it's important to physically release pent-up energy. Our bodies, like sponges, sop up tension into all of the their nooks and crannies. Screaming is a good physical release as long as it's not aimed at anyone and is done in private (screams can be muffled with a towel or pillow). Taking a run or brisk walk, beating a bed with a tennis racket, digging ferociously in the garden, and whacking tennis balls are all great stress siphons. You will know what's best for you. As long as physical release is not detrimental to yourself or anyone else, it usually helps clear a path to the heart.

Allowing our hearts to transform stress is the third step in siphoning it out of our bodies and souls. Move your awareness to your heart and visualize a symbol for the stress. Let the light and love of Spirit pour through you onto your symbol. Allow it to be transformed into peaceful energy. If it won't change, encase it in a container and put it on a remote shelf, and then surround yourself with a protective shield of light.

I am aware of stress and release it constructively.

I take stress into my heart, and bless and transform it with love and light.

Nourishing
Our Souls

*It is only when we can believe that
we are creating the soul that life has any
meaning, but when we can believe it—
and I do and always have—then there is
nothing we do that is without meaning and
nothing that we suffer that does not hold
the seed of creation in it.*

—May Sarton

WE EACH SEEK UNITY OF BODY, MIND, and spirit. As fundamentally spiritual beings living increasingly fragmented lives, we—even if we're not consciously aware of it—yearn to join the essentially complementary aspects of our being and integrate them into a balanced whole. I believe this yearning comes from deep within our souls as a memory of our life-purpose, which is that of achieving union between woman, who is finite, and spirit, which is infinite.

In order to have reconciliation of our human and spirit selves, both must be nourished and nurtured, befriended and given a voice. It is through the cleansed window of our humanity that our souls shine and become ever more visible. Because our humanity is loud and insistent while our spirit is quiet and patient, in the short run it's easier to "hop to" the worldly, physical demands and slight the whispers emanating from our spiritual selves. But, eventually, most of us, motivated by either a burning desire or an intermittent malaise, turn our attention to our souls and begin to heed their wisdom.

Daring to Breathe

DARING TO BREATHE IS ACTUALLY DARING TO live. As we all know, when we cease breathing, we die. As long as we are alive, the depth of our breathing determines the amount of life force we bring into ourselves. Given only a stingy amount of oxygen, our bodies, hearts, and minds will not function well.

When we are experiencing stress of any kind, our breathing has a tendency to get very shallow. As a therapist, I often need to remind my clients to breathe when they are working on issues. Often deeper breathing brings a release of tears and tension.

I was grateful the other day to notice a one-word bumper sticker: BREATHE, it prompted. *Breathe* is a reminder we need to give ourselves regularly. Breathing deeply brings more energy into our bodies, which, in turn, helps clarify both our thoughts and feelings.

Daring to breathe nourishes our souls as well. Almost all creation myths have God making man/woman from the soil of the earth and animating him/her by breathing into his/her nostrils the "breath of life." It's no wonder then that the words *soul* and *spirit* originated from *anima* and *spiritus*, both of which mean "breath." Through the grace of

God, we breathe, and it is the breath of God that we breathe. I find it very comforting to believe that God is as near to me as my next breath.

For the next five minutes, give yourself the life-enhancing gift of intentional breathing. With eyes closed, breathe deeply in through your nose, taking the breath of God—down, down into the center of your belly. Exhale completely through your mouth. As you inhale, imagine pure energy flowing in to nourish body and soul. As you exhale, let go of all that you would like to release.

If you get nothing else from *The Woman's Book of Soul*, I encourage you to make a commitment to breathe deeply five minutes a day—perhaps right before you get up or go to sleep. I think you'll be surprised and pleased at the profound changes that can occur from this one thing. Dare to do it!

Breathe!

I nourish body and soul by breathing deeply.

Going Where Gaia
Soothes Your Soul

. . . .

IT FEEDS OUR SPIRITS TO HAVE SPECIAL PLACES where Gaia, Mother Nature, can infuse us with her renewing energy. For me, it's the beach. While there, thoughts recede and worries abate. I could almost hang an UNOCCUPIED sign on my mind or stamp NOT AT THIS ADDRESS on my physical self. Even though I may not feel as if I've thought of a thing, as a result of being by the water, questions are often answered and decisions clarified. It's as if I've been mesmerized out of my own way, thereby freeing my spirit to do its wiser work.

Not all the insights that come up are peaches and cream. At the ocean, Gaia invites me to experience and release difficult feelings, especially grief—not as a head-trip, but rather at a more primal, accepting-the-natural-cycle-of-things way. Joy comes similarly. It's as if my soul gently surfs the waves and the movement quiets my human self. No matter what I feel or don't feel, I return from a time at the beach revived and rejuvenated. For me, a trip to the ocean is a trip to the eternal spring within myself.

Consider for a moment where your soul rests most easily. Where do you feel infinitely safe and return from replenished? What place in Mother Nature allows you to most readily hear the intuitive wisdom of your heart and seamlessly heal from searing wounds? It can be as exotic as a Polynesian beach or as accessible as your backyard. Even if you've only been to your special place once, you can always return in your imagination. If you don't have a sacred space in nature, be on the lookout for one and, until you find it, create one in your mind's eye.

Take a few quiet moments now to allow Gaia to nourish your soul. Imagine yourself in a grace-filled place and, as free of thought as possible, absorb the soothing energy. Breathe, relax, bask in nature's blessing.

I allow Gaia to soothe my soul.

Thank you, Mother Nature, for your blessings.

Being Our Own Lamp

AS HE WAS DYING, THE BUDDHA SAID, "BE A lamp unto yourself." I think he was challenging us to become aware of our spiritual essence, to read ourselves by our *own* light, to follow the path that resonates with our own hearts and minds right here, right now. As we recognize own unique light, we can choose to shine it on the people and places that need illuminating. For the good of the world, as well as our own personal good, it's vital that we tip over the proverbial bushel and become aware of the beautiful and distinctive light we have been given to share.

Settle yourself into a comfortable place and position and allow your breath to deepen naturally. With each breath, any tension that you are feeling begins to wane, drifting lazily and effortlessly out of your body as you exhale. The more you relax, the more you sink into the darkness behind your eyelids—a safe, embracing, womblike darkness wrapping around you like a soft comforter.

Stay here, safe and warm in the velvety darkness, as long as you like. At the right time for you, notice, in the distance, a small pinpoint of light. Gently and leisurely move toward the faint glow. Coming closer, you see that the light is emanating from an exquisite lamp resting atop a lamp stand. If you don't like the lamp that you see, allow it to fade and be replaced by one that feels right to you. Realizing that the lamp is a symbol of your unique inner light brought forth by your wise subconscious, ask it to share its wisdom with you. Listen carefully.

By the light of many lamps, much can be illuminated.

I am my own best light.
I share my love and light.

Resting in the Cradle of Friendship

IN ORDER FOR HER SPIRIT TO SOAR, A WOMAN needs the sense of security that close friendships provide. We need to be known and accepted for who we are and, at the same time, gently encouraged to become who we have the potential to be. When the soft feathers of friendship cradle our weary heads, we rest more easily and arise refreshed and ready to grow.

Ruth and Anne have been dear friends for almost twenty years. Although now separated by miles, they are committed to remaining united by fax, phone, and visits. Why is their connection so important to them? Because they truly *know* each other. Even though secrets and shame have been shared as readily as silliness and successes, their love and delight in each other continues to mature and ripen as they do.

"Sometimes I'm just starved to talk to and be with someone who knows me as well as I know them," Ruth once told Anne. She was voicing a common yearning in women. Being feminine, our ability to really know others often comes fairly naturally. It is one of our gifts, but a gift that we need to receive as well as give. We, too, need to be known. Being truly *known* and accepted, as is, can nourish our soul to new heights.

Right now, give yourself the gift of thinking about the special friendships that nourish you. Do you see or talk to these people enough to feel nourished? If you feel the lack of such trusted friendship, creatively play with what you can do to reach out and meet new people. It's perfectly okay to make a plan. Perhaps write a list of friends whom you would like to connect with more regularly and decide how to do so. Pencil them in and then follow through. You can make another plan for fostering new connections.

You will feel better when you fill the need to nourish yourself with the "soul food" of friendship.

I have a right to be known and accepted as I truly am.

I give myself the gift of friendship.

Culling Complications,
Welcoming Simplicity

. . . .

WE ARE CONTINUALLY SEDUCED BY SOCIETY
and our own need to do more, earn more, and
spend more into continuously complicating our
lives. Although some high-powered activity is stim-
ulating, even fun, and sometimes necessary, too
much is numbing and debilitating. The price many
of us pay for an overcomplicated existence is poor
health, loss of serenity, fractured relationships, and
an unspoken lament of, "Is this all there is?"

As a result of hard work and business acumen,
the company Sarah and her husband started in
their garage grew beyond their wildest imaginings.
With the growth, Sarah's responsibilities increased,
her private time all but ceased, and she had no
opportunity for relaxation. She assured herself and
friends that she was going to slow down—right
after this next trip, the coming ad campaign, or ad
infinitum. It wasn't until she woke up one morning
in excruciating pain, her shoulders and arms immobile, that Sarah realized she had to make changes.
She simply couldn't "shoulder" all the responsibilities she was carrying. Complication was literally
crippling her.

Sarah still works more than is totally comfortable, but she is also learning to delegate, set priorities, and simplify. She hired some help, turned down some projects, and pruned some acquaintances who were energy drains. Her life now includes solitude, gardening, time for friends and family, a regular meditation group, and daily exercise, all of which nourish her soul.

With great love and respect for yourself, gently but with absolute—and maybe life-saving—honesty, examine your life. Is it too complicated to be comfortable? If so, where can you simplify? What small step can you take today to welcome simplicity into your days and serenity into your nights?

A simpler life is frequently a more satisfying life.

I take responsibility for simplifying my life.

I am able to cull out complications.

Quieting the Mind

IT IS IN THE SILENCE OF A QUIET MIND THAT our spirits make themselves known to us. In the tranquility of a calm mind, we become aware of the murmurs of our soul and learn to appreciate the wisdom of our hearts. Indra Devi, author of *Renewing Your Life Through Yoga*, beautifully describes the quiet mind: "Like water, which can clearly mirror the sky and the trees only so long as its surface is undisturbed, the mind can only reflect the true image of the Self when it is tranquil and wholly relaxed. A ghost of wind—and the rippling waters will distort the reflection; a storm—and the reflection disappears altogether."

We are living in stormy times in which winds blow wildly across the waters of our minds and can all but obliterate our spiritual essence. But I know from personal experience that we can quiet both the storms and our minds. When I was younger, giant tsunamis regularly whipped the waters of my mind into a frenzy, rendering me deaf to my conscious wisdom, let alone the wisdom of my heart and soul. Although storms still ruffle my waters, remembering to breathe deeply and doing the following meditation helps the tempest to subside.

Close your eyes and gently allow your breath to deepen. Breathe in the idea of serenity and peace, and breathe out chaos and confusion. In your mind's eye, imagine a pond or lake that symbolizes your mind. Without judgment, notice how calm or turbulent it is and observe it for a minute. Ask your wise inner knowing what you can learn from this disturbance, and quietly listen. It doesn't matter if you "hear" an answer, trust that you will be made aware when the time is right. Now, breathe into your heart and, very deliberately, still the wind across the water. Breathe deeply until the lake is tranquil. Look at your reflection and thank yourself for calming the storm.

A quiet mind can reflect the real you.

Each day I become calmer and clearer.
I am a clear reflection of the Divine Spirit.

Unplugging the Phone

IN A MOVIE REVIEW I READ RECENTLY, THE reviewer said, "This movie shows that our world may not end with a bang or a whimper but with a busy signal." What an apt metaphor! Our lives are busy, our phones and faxes are busy, our kids are busy, our friends are busy, our mates are busy, and our minds are busy. With these interminable busy signals, how can our souls ever contact us?

Joni is a friend of mine who never answers the phone but lets the answering machine be her vigilant secretary. She says it saves her a tremendous amount of time and energy, because she is the one who decides when she feels like talking and can call people back when she's ready.

Unplugging the literal telephone may not be feasible—I for one am too curious to let the phone ring, and for many of us the phone is our livelihood. But what about the busy signals in our lives? Do our kids get a busy signal when they need our attention? How about the little kids we all carry around inside of us; can they get through to us? Very importantly, are the bearers of our intuitive, heart-wisdom able to get our attention, or are they, too, frustrated by a continuous busy signal?

Interestingly, the loudest, most incessant buzzers demanding our attention can also be the least nourishing to our souls, but we answer them out of habit or a sense of obligation. I'm sure you can think of a few annoying and energy-wasting distractions. Solicitors who call during the dinner hour spring to mind. One simple way to eliminate some of the busyness from our lives is to "turn off the ringer" on superfluous demands. Doing so gives us more opportunity to connect with ourselves and those we love.

It may sound mundane, but unplugging from only a few distractions can make us feel much freer. Experiment by cutting the connection to only one thing that is an energy drain for you and see how it feels.

I eliminate the unimportant.

I have enough time and attention to give to that which is important to me.

Honoring Our Own Rhythm

"I GOT RHYTHM, YOU GOT RHYTHM, ALL GOD'S children got rhythm," declares the spiritual. True, but we women regularly allow ourselves to be pulled from our own rhythm into another's, and we are especially prone to subjugate our rhythm to those of our mates and children. Luckily, we are also incredibly adaptable and can modify our rhythm to others for fairly long periods of time without adverse effects.

However, endlessly disregarding our inner music eventually causes us to literally be out of step with ourselves. A few of the resultant feelings may be irritation, depression, restlessness, and resentment. When we experience these, it's time to dance to our own drummer and find ways to honor our unique rhythm.

I experienced being very out-of-sync not long ago. Worn out from long writing sessions and a burst of author-on-tour promotional trips, and thoroughly exhausted from emoting both in person and on paper, I was not my nicest person. Luckily for him, my husband had planned a trip out of town. Alone and assisted by a bout of food poisoning, my life slowed to about one-third of its normal pace.

I turned down most offers to socialize, but at one gathering that I needed to attend people commented on how "beautiful" I looked and wondered if I'd had plastic surgery. A rather backhanded compliment, but never having borne the label of beautiful—especially not since the "crone years" started—I accepted their comment gladly. Upon reflection, I think the beauty these people saw was a result of the relaxation, ease, and comfort I felt at being in my own rhythm for those few days.

We all need to rest, retreat, and replenish. Pay attention to your body and soul signals and find your own unique and precious rhythm, if not for days, then for hours or minutes today. What does paying attention to your rhythm teach you? Are there any small changes in yours that you could make to accommodate yourself? The rhythm to which our spirit can best dance is the rhythm of Self.

I know, appreciate, and allow my own rhythm.

Each day I take some time to be in my personal rhythm.

Tending the Temple

. . . .

OUR BODIES ARE AMAZINGLY MIRACULOUS
temples that house our souls and allow us to have
this existence. They are the vehicles through
which we express ourselves while they instinctively
perform trillions of functions that keep us up and
running. But, like Rodney Dangerfield, they often
"don't get no respect" from us.

As Walt Whitman made clear when he wrote, "If
life and the soul are sacred, the human body is
sacred," we need to realize the sanctity of our
body-temple and make it a priority to tend to it res-
ponsibly and respectfully. When the body is too
tired, malnourished, overworked, stressed out, or
lacks enough exercise, it begins to falter system by
system. Because the body/spirit connection is so
strong, in some real sense, ignoring our body is a
spiritual emergency; we have ravaged our temple.

Realizing our need to tend the temple is especially hard when we're in a caregiver role (and who
of us is not, in some form or another?). Betty was
the primary caretaker for her terminally ill husband. While she carefully prepared meals for him,
she existed on snacks and coffee. Although she
used to walk daily, she no longer felt she could
leave the house unless it was on a necessary errand.
Her daughter, visiting from out of town, was

appalled at her mother's appearance. "You look worse than Dad!" she cried, and then set about helping Betty find regular help from her church and hospice. From her daughter's reaction, Betty learned an important lesson; taking care of Self is so easy to forget and so necessary to remember.

For a moment, close your eyes and visualize a temple that symbolizes your body right now. Don't be alarmed if it looks ramshackled. The first time I did this visualization, my temple looked like the remnants of an old treehouse. Learn from the image that your wise subconscious presents. Ask your temple what it wants and needs in order to feel healthy and energetic.

If our body houses our soul, can it peek through the clutter or get our attention amid the chaos?

I treat my body as I would a dear friend.
My body is the sacred temple of my soul.

Steering Clear of Black Holes

I WAS TALKING TO A WISE YOUNG WOMAN named Laurie about relationships, and she made a statement that I've never forgotten: "I try to make sure that in all of my important relationships there is an even exchange of energy." Laurie's philosophy struck at the very heart of an issue I was wrestling with concerning a friendship with two women. I was usually with these women in a group of four, and I always felt weird during and after a gathering.

Laurie's comment came at the time when I was chastising myself harshly for feeling uncomfortable in these friendships. As a therapist, I know all about projection of our unconscious feelings onto other people, and I worked with myself about the possibility that I was doing that. But no little subconscious worms were unearthed in all of my digging, so I examined my feelings by the light of Laurie's statement and realized that there was no *exchange* of energy. The energy I put out to these two women was merely absorbed as if it had disappeared into a black hole and none came back to me.

There are some perfectly wonderful people who, mysteriously, are virtual black holes for our energy. We send scads of energy and attention their way, and it just disappears. Nothing comes back. Zero, zip! If we're saddled with the belief that everyone needs to like us in order for us to be acceptable or that we should be able to be friends with anyone, we can cause ourselves a lot of pain. We're simply "energetic misses" with some people. We're not bad, they're not bad; we just don't fit.

If you are in a relationship that feels one-sided and believe that you must continue it in order to be a nice person, for your own good let go of that belief. First, examine the possibility that you're projecting your "own stuff," and then trust your wise intuition. If it seems right, give yourself permission to move out of Black Hole Territory.

We have too little time to waste it in relationships that are not equal and mutually rewarding. *Exchanging* energy nourishes our souls—black holes enervate rather than energize them.

I choose relationships in which energy is exchanged equally.

It's perfectly okay not to hit it off with absolutely everyone.

Surrendering to Tiredness

SURRENDER TO TIREDNESS! THE IDEA IS A TOUGH one to assimilate, isn't it? Of course it is a hard concept to grasp, because it isn't the way we've been trained to act. It's true that women have incredible stamina and can do it all for a while, but there is the reality of accumulated fatigue. After a certain amount of outpouring, we are just plain bone-weary. To nourish both our souls and our bodies, we need to surrender to tiredness before it becomes exhaustion and our wise body has no recourse but to knock the pegs out from under us via illness, incompetence, or debilitating depression.

Not long after our daughter's wedding, I was feeling like a beige dishrag. No energy, no enthusiasm, no feelings of love; just a gray void. Longing to know why my zest for life was at zero and falling, I meditated and then wrote questions to whom I hoped would be the wise person within me. Two of my questions were: "Why don't I feel anything?" and "Why are there so many tears as I write this?"

The answer I wrote to myself was this: *The tears are tiredness. You have been holding—even making—the space for everyone in your family and extended family. You are allowed to rest. That is grace. Remember, even the church statues are draped during Holy Week. Even they are allowed* to rest. *So rest, my dear. This is your holy time, and much is synthesizing on different levels in dreams, and so on. Sit, rest, replenish.* It was such a profound message for me that, even as I write this now, tears have welled up and I realize again how much I resist surrendering to tiredness.

If you are a woman who easily surrenders to tiredness, I congratulate you. If you are like me and find it difficult, then, together, let us give each other permission right now to rest and replenish in the perfect, right ways for us.

I have the right and responsibility to rest and replenish myself.

I know when I am tired and allow myself to rest.

Sending Guilt Down the Drain

GUILT SUCKS OUR SOULS DRY. A TINY TINGE OF guilt can be appropriate and even helpful if we use it as a warning signal—"Whoops, wrong way. Wait, do I really want to say/do that?" But most of us use the guilt-as-sledge-hammer approach and let it bludgeon us until we're black and blue.

After a discussion with her new husband in which he told her that he was having a very hard time with her "freeloader" eighteen-year-old son, Marcie told the boy that he needed to move out. Almost immediately she was aware that she didn't want him to leave and that telling him to do so had been an attempt to appease her husband. On the heels of the ultimatum, Marcie and her husband went square dancing. "Well," she said, "Guilt can't dance!" How right she is. Guilt hobbles us almost more than any emotion, and 94 percent (I just made that number up, but I'm probably close) of the guilt we take on is either inappropriate or not ours in the first place. Guilt-grabbing is one of women's lesser talents.

Alice, a client of mine and a recovering guilt-grabber, shared a wonderful ritual with me that she came up with as a part of her self-therapy. When she notices that she is "slimed with guilt," as she put it, she hops in the shower as soon as possible and uses a loofah sponge to scrub herself down. During the scouring, she affirms that she is freeing herself of guilt and visualizes it swirling away down the drain to be transmuted into perfect, righteous energy. If she's aware of what they are, she also scrubs off the old roles and beliefs she's held that led to this particular bout of guilt. The pièce de résistance is a rousing rendition of "I'm gonna wash that guilt right out of myself," which she sings at the top of her lungs.

I've tried Alice's technique and you might want to also. It's fun and lightens up the heaviness guilt can assume.

I let go of guilt effortlessly.

I am a good person even though I make mistakes.

Designing Sacred Space

BECAUSE A WOMAN IS SO SENSITIVE TO THE nuances of the space around her, her home needs to nourish her soul. We thrive best in a nest that is both a shelter in which to retreat and a launching pad from which to soar.

Each of us has different tastes and needs. What feels sacred to one may jangle another's nerves. We may want our entire house to feel sacred, or a small altar or a modest corner of a garden may suffice perfectly. One of my friends has a private little room chock full of hummingbird symbols where she goes and "breathes a sigh of relief." Another woman's entire home is decorated in vibrant Mexican decor, which soothes her soul; yet another's retreat is a tiny garden under a favorite tree.

In order to figure out how to create sacred space for yourself, take a thoughtful and leisurely stroll through your house and yard. Is there a room, a particular piece of furniture, or a small space that whispers to you, "Welcome home . . . Come, sit here, and relax. Rest, create, dream, plan, worship . . ."? In space that feels sacred to us, we sigh with relief and soar more effortlessly into our soul selves. We are home. If, on your tour, you find a spot that calls to you, how would you like to augment it? If you don't find a favorite "home" spot, meditate on what it might look like if you did create a sacred space. It will come to you. When we look into our hearts, we know what sort of space nourishes our souls and replenishes our inner resources.

We deserve and *need* for our homes, or special places within them, to reflect our essence. Gift yourself with sacred space.

I give myself permission to create sacred spaces around me.

My home reflects and nourishes my soul.

Intertwining
Soul-Strands

And remember, we all stumble, every one of us.
That's why it's a comfort to go hand in hand.

—E. K. Brough

B EING IN A RELATIONSHIP IS OUR MOST valuable spiritual workshop. Relationships are the threads with which God weaves our earthly world, and the ways we care for and communicate with ourselves and each other create the patterns for our lives.

When we intertwine our soul-strands with others, we are brought face-to-face with our deepest fears and our highest aspirations. We are catapulted to towering heights and dragged to numbing depths, all in the service of soul.

I will admit that, on occasion, I have thought that a simple, solitary spiritual path would be just dandy. Leave me alone, and I'll come home to God wagging—not dragging—my tail behind me. But, in reality, we are relational beings who want and need to be connected to others in meaningful ways, no matter what joys and sorrows are involved. Allowing ourselves to intertwine soul-strands provides us with ample opportunities to love and be loved, and love is the path to Spirit.

Weaving Our Souls Together

EACH OF US HAS MUCH TO LEARN FROM relating to others. Because they know us so well, our mates, children, and close friends are often our most resourceful teachers. While this truth may be self-evident, it is frequently difficult at any given moment for us to be good students.

One way to become an eager, or at least a willing, pupil is to realize that we intertwine our soul strands with those of our intimates when we agree to be in relationships. From the weaving together of our individual spirits emerges a much larger picture, that of our soul's work, both individually and jointly.

Keeping that larger soul perspective is vital, especially when things are difficult between us. Remembering our soul connection helps enable us to act from and with love.

To get an image of this joining, sit quietly with your eyes closed and meditate on a relationship between you and a loved one. Allow positive energy to flow from your heart to the other person's. See or imagine your soul-strands rising from the top of your heads. Watch as those beautiful and unique soul-strands weave together, dancing to the music that only your relationship can compose. Delight in the joy of your souls' harmony.

Visualizing like this helps us rise above some of the human issues that often cloud our higher sight, and it allows us to travel into the realm of insight about our soul's commitment of the heart.

I deserve to dance to the music of love.
I weave my heart and soul with those I love.

Making Conscious Connections

COMMUNICATION IS AT THE HEART OF OUR lives and connects our souls with those we love and with the soul of the world. How we communicate determines whether we build bridges or create chasms within ourselves, and between ourselves, others, the environment, and God. If our communication with ourselves is a continual crucifixion, our spirits become wounded and clamp tightly shut. A closed spirit cannot commune with others, soul to soul.

Artful communication, on the other hand, connects us to ourselves and each other, bonds us together through strands of energy, actions, and words. At best, communication becomes a daily communion, in which we express the highest and deepest within us, and share the very best of ourselves, thereby calling forth the very best from others.

We are constantly, intuitively, and innately communicating. But do we communicate *consciously*? To communicate from our hearts and souls, we need to commit ourselves to being aware of how, why, and even when we communicate. Learning to consciously communicate will help us understand what our intention is during any particular encounter, especially during times of intense emotion and vulnerability. If our intention is to win, or to be right, we'd better pause until we can change that to a desire for better understanding and connection.

Consciously communicating means that you ask yourself if what you're saying enhances feelings of affinity, safety, and connection in your relationships. If the answer is consistently a yes, you are a valuable teacher and model for supportive relationships, and I am thankful for you. While most of us communicate consciously sometimes, because we are all so vulnerable, we truly need to learn to communicate consciously most, if not all, of the time.

Conscious, artful communication is a sacrament of love, support, and safety that deepens our connections to others.

My goals in communicating are
understanding and connection.

I am thoughtful about what I say and do.

Cleansing Your Personal Vase

COMMUNICATION IS THE SACRED VESSEL FROM which we pour the wine of our souls into our lives and relationships. Because of this, we need to clean up any habits that may be tainting the wine. Major poisoning comes from the sludge of self-criticism and chastisement that we often pour on ourselves.

Habitually treating ourselves poorly and severely judging what we do and say causes our spirits to retreat in confusion and fear. In order to express the good, true, and beautiful within us, we must remember to communicate with ourselves gently. It's so important that we speak to ourselves as a dear and cherished friend and are encouraging and supportive within the privacy of our own minds. Doing so helps us evolve into being loving and patient with others as well as ourselves. It is possible to learn to do. I know because I had the dirtiest vessel imaginable when I was younger, and vinegar, not wine, gushed from it onto myself primarily. Most of the whispers of my mind were like daggers in my heart. That's no longer true, and, although changing the pattern was not easy and took commitment and effort, it was well worth the struggle.

In order to break any pattern of verbal self-abuse, we need to be on the lookout for detrimental self-talk and replace it immediately with communication worthy of a soul-friend. To help yourself succeed, close your eyes and invite the image of a vase to come into the theater of your mind. Ask that it symbolize the vessel of communication between you and yourself. Envision your self-talk being poured into this vase. Is it pure and supportive, or clouded and discouraging?

As you are pondering your vase, become aware of the soft sound of water. Looking around, notice a small but beautiful waterfall gently cascading into a crystal pool. Cleanse your vase in it, and, when it is clean, fill it with the wine of your spirit, which pours from the pristine center of your soul.

I am a beloved child of God.

I speak to myself with love and respect.

Awakening the Sleeping Spirit

AS HAPPENED TO SLEEPING BEAUTY, A POSSESsive and jealous fairy (whom I call the world fairy) can cast her spell on us sometime in childhood, and as we move into the responsibilities of adulthood, we fall asleep. Doing the "stuff" of grownups, we work, play, raise families, have friends, and volunteer our services, but all too often our spiritual connections drift into somnolence. Basically, we fall asleep at the wheel and forget to relate to the soul of ourselves or our loved ones.

Luckily, we have within us a different kind of fairy, an intrinsic soul fairy, who communes with us continuously. She is soft-spoken and gentle, but persistent. A devoted friend to our spirits, she whispers inspirations and songs of love into our ears. We catch hints of her lyrics and melodies every day, but are often too sleepy or busy to pay attention. Not to worry, because her songs are eternal, and she will still be singing when our thirsty souls convince us to pay attention.

We can quiet our minds to be able to hear her songs through meditation. Meditation is listening to the Divine within, and our soul fairy is a wonderful spokesbeing for the Divine. Let's use her now as an entry through the door of meditation.

With your eyes closed, allow your breath to

deepen into a comfortable rhythm. Picture your soul fairy and imagine her giving you a word to use during this meditation. Listen carefully, but without stress or expectation, and allow a word, or short series of words, to float easily into your awareness. Words that often come to me are "Thank You," and "You through me." One friend tenderly says, "Wake up, Spirit." Breathe your words either into your heart center or into your tummy. If your mind wanders off, gently return your attention to your breath and the word or words.

Each time we practice this meditation, we move deeper and deeper into our center, where the Divine sits beside our spirit, which longs to be awakened.

I listen for the songs of my soul fairy.
I invite my spirit to be fully awake.

Listening Deeply

. . . .

TO THE SACRED FEMININE VOICE OF OUR hearts, listening is a sacred art. Deeply listening is miraculous for both listener and speaker. When someone welcomes us with open-hearted, accepting, interested listening, our spirits expand and we are inspired to unveil the miracle of our Self.

The Yiddish proverb "There is no one as deaf as he who will not listen" speaks simply to a basic truth. We have an epidemic of deafness in our world, and the result of not hearing one another in a meaningful way is a profound and poignant loneliness. As plants shrivel without sun and water, we are dying in spirit for lack of deep listening.

The words *heart* and *listen* provide hints about the art of listening deeply. *Heart* contains within it the word *hear*, and *listen* contains the exact same letters as *silent*. In order to hear what is being said and felt, we need to be silent and listen from our hearts; we must close our mouths and give undivided attention to others when they open theirs.

I watched a young mother do this beautifully when her three-year-old son began to continuously interrupt our conversation. She excused herself from me and looked directly in his eyes. "Do you need a little UDA?" she asked. For me, she clarified, "Undivided attention." He said that he did, and this wise mom totally turned her attention to her son, listening deeply. After about five minutes of UDA, he jumped down from the table saying, "Okay, I'm done" and went off to play. Miracle accomplished.

When we practice the sacred art of listening, we intertwine our souls. Deep listening from the heart of the Sacred Feminine fosters understanding, and understanding can miraculously turn into love.

I listen deeply to others.
I listen from my heart.

Letting Love Flow

THERE ARE TIMES WHEN OUR COMMITMENT TO our loved ones is more a decision than a feeling. When that is the case, we can allow *agape*, or the impersonal love of the Divine, to flow *through* us to them. Yielding to God's love flowing through, instead of relying on our own abilities to send unconditional regard, is especially necessary for the times that we do not, on a human level, give one roaring toot whether this totally icky other person is loved or not.

When I was angrily sloughing through the quagmire of my divorce, Annabelle, my spiritual mother and mentor, taught me to sit quietly with my eyes closed and begin a positive flow of energy from my heart to another's by imagining the recipient of my energy stream as someone or something that I felt absolutely loving toward. Often I used one of my children, a puppy, or a flower.

When the heart flow was solidly established, very, very slowly I let the picture fade and allowed the image of my former husband to take its place. If the flow stopped, I would put the easier recipient back in place and begin the exercise again. I was really doing this more for me than for him, because I knew that the rage and hate I was experiencing were blocking my ability to open fully to love.

When we block our love to and from another person, we cut off our own energy supply from our spirit-selves. We are short-circuited. As soon as we can restore harmony in ourselves and reactivate our willingness to send unconditional regard (it's perfectly all right if it is *impersonal*), love energy begins to flow back into us from our higher self, and then out to the other person. A closed heart can neither give nor receive, while an open heart is a direct conduit for the Beloved to love through us.

I allow love to flow through me.
I can love even difficult people impersonally.

Neutralizing Knee-Jerks

BECAUSE WE ARE HUMAN, WE ALL HAVE KNEE-jerk reactions—most of which are negative—to certain situations or provocations. But reactions often need to be reviewed or they can shred the dickens out of relationships and our own self-esteem. As the wise Chinese proverb states, "If you are patient in one moment of anger, you will escape a hundred days of sorrow." That's because acting on our knee-jerk responses usually ends up causing us to feel sorrow, guilt, and/or shame. When we go for the jugular, everyone gets bloodied.

Knee-jerk reactions are automatic, out-of-soul responses, and, although we may not stop ourselves from having them, we definitely can stop ourselves from expressing them. Knee-jerks inevitably land on someone else, and disconnection is the result. Separation doesn't draw us closer to each other or to the core of our Selves.

Tricia, a young client of mine, had fractured several relationships with very nice young men because, during emotional encounters, she blurted out whatever came into her mind. Usually, it was hurtful. Being subjected to her venomous strikes eventually caused the men to leave.

After much denial, Tricia finally realized that her wounding, uncontrolled responses were the culprits that kicked the men out of her life. This awareness was the beginning of her ongoing work to neutralize her sabotaging knee-jerk reactions.

If we are to keep our relationships safe havens for soul-growth and self-expression, we need to neutralize knee-jerks. The old adage of counting to ten is based on pure wisdom.

Today, if something happens to provoke you, pause. Move into your heart. Count if it helps, and excuse yourself for a time-out if you need it. Become aware of your breath. During conflict our breath becomes very shallow. Consciously deepen your breathing and ask yourself how you choose to respond. We DO have the choice, and our choices determine whether we connect with others soulfully or experience "a hundred days of sorrow."

I carefully choose my responses.

When upset or confused, I pause and breathe.

Wising Up in the Silence

WISDOM AND INTUITION ARE BIRTHED IN silence. Before you read on, take a few moments to close your eyes and relax into the hush of silence. Neither asking nor expecting anything of yourself, merely relax into the quietness.

For some of us, it takes practice to feel comfortable with silence, although I believe all of us intuitively understand its value. One of the reasons that it's very important is that only in silence can we hear the feminine energy of our hearts.

If we listen closely in the silence, the Sacred Feminine will show us how to lovingly intertwine soul-strands in our relationships with others and with ourselves. Our relationships can hum with the songs of love only if they are filled with the Sacred Feminine Voice, for she *is* the song of love. She is the harp upon which the strings of compassion and connection quiver. From the Sacred Feminine comes the sweet music composed by living complementary lives with those we love.

"Silence is the language of God; it is also the language of the heart," said Danish statesman and philosopher, Dag Hammarskjöld. The more faithfully we move into the silence, the more attuned we will become to the voice of Spirit.

Today, give yourself the gift of relaxing into the

silence. Softly, gently, lovingly allow silence to immerse you in peace. As a result, the music of wisdom and intuition will become clearer and more harmonious.

I relax into the silence today.

I allow the Sacred Feminine to teach me about love.

Communicating Love Through Action

Thought is the blossom,
Language the bud,
Action the fruit behind it.

—R. W. Emerson

IT'S EASY TO SPEAK OF LOVE AND CARING, BUT not so easy to match our actions to the words. The old adage "actions speak louder than words" is absolutely true because, when we can be counted on to do as we say we will, trust is the by-product. Relationships thrive on trust. In fact, it's best to intimately intertwine our soul-strands only with those whom we can trust implicitly. Those are the alliances that will feed our spirits. Whether a caring relationship is close or casual, we need to be able to count on the integrity of ourselves and others.

Being extremely busy when it came time to move her office, Bonnie told the woman who owned and operated the moving company "Just pack it and take it to this address." After a difficult day at another office, Bonnie dragged herself to the new place, harried, exhausted, and dreading the thought of unpacking. She opened the door to a sweet surprise—everything was unpacked and arranged *exactly* as it had been in the old office, down to the sea-shells on the shelves. In the face of such caring by her from-the-heart movers, tears of gratitude flowed, and the remnants of a horrible week seemed to be washed away with them.

Our actions inevitably communicate our true love quotient. What close or casual relationship would benefit from the fruit of action from you? How can you, today, communicate love through action either to yourself or to another?

I match my actions to my words.

I and other people can count on me.

Speaking with Spirit-Tongue

IN ORDER TO KEEP THE THREADS THAT WEAVE us together from fraying, we need to speak our truth and resolve conflicts within a container of caring. I am able to do this much more consistently when I remember the Four Noble Truths. The wisdom of the four noble truths can be found in many cultures, but I'm sharing knowledge found in The Great Wheel of Life, an ancient circular symbol that has been used by native peoples for thousands of years, and augmented by anthropologist Angeles Arrien and me.

The Four Noble Truths are:

1. SHOW UP and choose to be present to all that life offers. Be a good model—by walking your talk.

2. PAY ATTENTION to what has heart and meaning for you and resonates within your soul.

3. TELL THE TRUTH without blame or judgment. Say what you mean and mean what you say (indigenous peoples call this "speaking with spirit-tongue") or, KEEP NOBLE SILENCE. From an empowered position, choose to remain silent.

4. STAY OPEN, BUT NOT ATTACHED TO THE OUTCOME. Deeply care, from an objective place. Break old patterns. Practice discernment.

If we did nothing else but adopt and live these four wonderful truths, our spirits would soar to new heights and our relationships would be healthy and holy. Remembering that the bottom line needs to be drawn with love, we can choose to speak with spirit-tongue or maintain noble silence.

I never speak with the intention of hurting.

I honor my truth and speak it caringly.

Enlivening with Enthusiasm

ENTHUSIASM COMES FROM THE GREEK *enthousiasmos* and means "having a God within" or "possessed by a divine spirit." I love that! Since our enthusiasm is linked to the God within, to our Divine Spirit, it's incredibly important that we endorse rather than drown fiery excitement.

Many of us have had our enthusiasm dampened as children. Although no one may have purpose-fully set out to squelch us, it undoubtedly happened, at least on occasion. If we've been silenced, cautioned to "calm down" or, worse yet, put down when enthusiastic, it's even more important for us to tend the fire of enthusiasm within ourselves and others. Doing so will help ignite, or reignite, the divine spark ever- present within our souls.

Close your eyes and allow yourself to sink deeply into the very center of your being. Focus on your breath and encourage it to become slower and deeper. If your mind is chattering, gently turn your attention to your breath and concentrate on draw-ing it into your heart center. Imagine that it is a lit-tle after twilight and you are sitting comfortably in front of a small campfire at the edge of a woods. Over the trees a luminous full moon is rising.

To your delighted surprise, you see a beautiful Being walking down a shaft of moonlight into your circle. With complete candor, you begin to share with this Being your dreams, aspirations, and just-plain-fun ideas. She listens with unbounded enthusiasm as she lovingly builds up the campfire as the night becomes cooler. Bask in the warmth of her attention and enthusiasm for your thoughts. Feel yourself becoming inspired and creative as a result.

Today, if only for a few minutes, allow yourself to be possessed by a divinely enthusiastic spirit. Search out at least one thing about which you can unabashedly gush. I bet you'll be surprised how infectious your excitement is to others and how energized you feel as a result.

I am alive with enthusiasm.

I greet my own and others' ideas and inspirations with enthusiasm.

Aligning Our Breath

. . . .

OUR RELATIONSHIPS WITH EACH OTHER AND with ourselves are bound to have some difficult moments. We are all vulnerable human beings who will, on occasion, have our feelings hurt. Or we may find ourselves in very painful situations without a clue regarding how to connect with someone, be helpful to them, or even cope ourselves.

Since all living things share breath, in difficult times often the best thing we can possibly do is to breathe together in silence. The following technique helps bring us into alignment with each other and intertwines our soul-strands in a very simple, compassionate way. You can even do it without the other person knowing it.

Without fuss or bother, gently begin to align your breath to the breath of the person with whom you are relating, following his or her rhythm of inhales and exhales. As you match him or her, ask the Beloved within you to help you listen from your heart to any spoken or unspoken message, and then open to hear the still, small voice of love.

I learned this method from a hospice nurse who worked exclusively with AIDS patients. She said that there were many days when, other than making her patients as comfortable as possible, all she could do was hold them and align her breath with theirs. More often than not, few words were uttered, but there were many tears shed. Tears of all kinds—sadness, frustration, guilt and shame, empathy, compassion, and spiritual joy—overflowed from nurse and patient as she gifted them with her presence and matching breath and they gifted her with their real, and often, luminous feelings.

We can align our breath to augment wonderful feelings as well as assuage troubling ones. Breathe rhythmically with your lover before making love. Duplicate a child's breath as you play together or as they sleep. Be creative and remember that as we align our breath, we align the very soul-strand that is inherent to us all.

I align my breath with those I want to connect with deeply.

My breath connects me to all living beings.

Honoring Sacred Rights and Responsibilities

The true Light is a gentle love which,
rising in you, causes you to look on the
world with understanding and compassion
and respect. When you respect the souls of
your brother and sister, you respect their
lives in every way. This gentle spirit, this
respect one for another, must come. For this
is the generation of the one true Light,
and this true light is that of love.

—*White Eagle*

THE FEMININE SPIRIT NOURISHES AND gives birth not only to other humans but ideas and ideals as well. As modern women, we are called to nourish and give birth to the light of gentle love and respect for all people. It is our sacred right and responsibility to realize that we, each and every one of us, is the fulfillment of Divine purpose. Ours are the hearts through which God's love flows; ours are the arms that hold the wounded, weary, and frightened; ours are the voices that can espouse understanding, tolerance, and compassion.

To be equal to the calling of the Spirit within and around us, we need to recognize that we already *are* who we need to be. Of course, as a natural part of our soul's refining process, we all have fears, false beliefs, and wounds to transform. But beneath the layers of humanity, we are whole. We don't get the holy grail—we are the grail. At our core, we are a cup from which God longs to pour love upon her children. Our sacred mission is to live in a state of love and integrity with ourselves first, and then pour the balm of love and integrity onto our thirsty world.

Living Gently with Yourself and Others

. . . .

AN IRISH PROVERB STATES A SIMPLE TRUTH, "Even a small thorn causes pain." How often, out of thoughtlessness or lack of attention, do we inflict pain, even though we don't want or mean to? We yearn to live gently, and yet gentleness—especially toward ourselves—seems so difficult in our fast-paced lives. When we are frantically trying to abide by a timetable that is at odds with our natural ebb and flow, the ability to breathe deeply and choose our reaction is diminished. Before we know it, a thorny comment is automatically launched.

Lost in the acceleration of our pace is the energy and time for gently supporting and nurturing ourselves and our loved ones. But with intention, we *can* cultivate the art of gentleness. However, we will need to make a strong commitment to living gently and adopt an *attitude* that supports our resolution. And as usual, we'll need to start this attitude adjustment by treating *ourselves* gently. What a thought!

Of course we expect ourselves to be gentle with others, but aren't we supposed to be our own hardest taskmaster and severest critic? No. In reality, learning to be gentle with ourselves enhances our ability to shine the light of love, trust, and respect on others. Embraced by a nurturing, sensitive *self*, we are better and safer friends and family members. Treating ourselves harshly bruises our hearts, and a bruised heart is more likely to treat others in a bruising way or at least wish it could.

I believe that we sincerely want to be gentle, but often don't know how. Sometimes all we need to adopt a gentle attitude is some small reminders. What would be a good reminder for you? Maybe a three-by-five card on the refrigerator saying, *Live gently with yourself and others*. Or an agreement with a friend to ask, "Is that gentle?" when you're hard on yourself. Take a few minutes today to give yourself and those you love a soul-enhancing gift—think of ways to welcome the art of gentleness into your life.

I live gently with myself and others.
Without judgment, I remind myself to be gentle.

Transforming Fear

MANY OF US FEEL A NEED TO CLIMB OUT OF THE black holes of fear into which we have been pushed or have leapt of our own accord—never to be afraid again. It's unreasonable to expect that we can evolve to a point where we never experience fear, but it is perfectly reasonable to believe that we can free ourselves from the limitations fear imposes, so that it neither dictates how we live nor totally distracts us from our spiritual path.

We are born with only two natural fears—fear of falling and fear of loud noises. All other fears are learned. If we learned them, we can *un*learn them. And unlearn them we must, for fear blocks out love and love is the vehicle for Spirit. That's why, as our fear is transformed, we are able to access more of our soul-spark, which is powerfully gentle, strong, and wise. Feminine qualities are desperately needed to create a safe and harmonious world.

Wanda, a client of mine, was so fearful that she couldn't leave her house to come to my office. So, for a short while, I went to her. With great effort and courage, Wanda began to track down the fearful beliefs buried within her psyche. Her most debilitating fear came from being the only daughter in a family of three brothers. As a product of the boys-are-better society, Wanda's mother unwittingly led her to believe that she wasn't as good as her brothers and could never do anything right.

Haunted by the fear that she actually had no right to exist, Wanda increasingly limited her life until she *wasn't* really living. Becoming aware of the fears she'd learned at (and sometimes over) her mother's knee, Wanda began to disentangle herself from them through therapy and dedicated work. The day she finally walked through my office door was one of celebration.

Like Wanda, there are times when we can't do it alone. If you feel at a loss, please be gentle with yourself and seek help. Fear transformed translates into empowerment and love. GREAT!

I have the wisdom to seek help.
I have the courage to unlearn fears.

Evolving into Simplicity

HUMAN CONSCIOUSNESS IS EVER-EVOLVING. Actually *everything* is always evolving, and, interestingly, evolution is not toward more complexity as we might suspect but toward *simplicity*. That is why our souls thirst for simplicity; in their wisdom, they know that love and spirit are simple.

While talking to Debra, a recently widowed friend, I was struck by her answer to my question, "Were the last few weeks of Todd's illness very difficult for your family?" Surprisingly, she answered, "No. By then we all knew that he would die, and we lived moment-to-moment. Our life was trimmed down to the simplest things—a tiny smile, a drink of water, flashes of deep heart connection through feeling or even a little talking. It was the simplest and the *sweetest* time of my life." Wow!

Debra's comments resonated with an almost wordless thirst within me. Simplicity. Sweetness. Time for reflection and relating. Umm . . . The upshot of that conversation is a deep commitment on my part to trim the unnecessary and the unwanted from my life without there having to be a crisis to provoke it, and to get progressively better at discerning when less is more. Sort of a continous soul garage sale.

Right now, gently, and with great compassion,

take a deep breath and look at your calendar for the next week. If it is more crowded than you feel comfortable with, ponder what activities and obligations may be unnecessary or unwanted. Without judgment, ask yourself if you are an "automatic yes'er." Do you say yes even if you feel no?

Are you thirsty for the solace of simplicity? If so, tuck in your heart and mind a promise to evolve into more simplicity. Start by eliminating just one tiny or tremendous thing that feels unnecessary or unwanted. Simplicity can be simply and soulfully wonderful.

Simple is as simple doesn't.

I am creating a simple and sweet lifestyle that is right for me.

Balancing on the Cusp

WE ARE ON THE BRINK OF A SPIRITUAL renaissance in our post-industrial world, poised on the cusp of a new paradigm that has endless possibilities for new beginnings. In ever-growing numbers, we are becoming aware of an ancient, mysterious, spiritual reality of oneness. This mystery was never mysterious to mystics and indigenous peoples who intuitively lived with the awareness that we are all linked together—people, plants, and animals—as creations of the Divine.

In our culture, however, we have been saturated with the almost universal belief in *separateness*, not oneness, which is why it is sometimes hard for us to see how we are related. It's true that we look separate, but if we could see the energy fields within and emanating from us, we would see that our energy intermingles with all energies: trees, teenagers, Tasmanians, tantrum-throwing tots. Everyone, everything.

It's an awesome idea, isn't it? It can also be a scary idea if our security rests in being separate and/or superior, or in being *sure* of the rules and realities. Nonetheless, energetic oneness is an actuality discovered by scientific research and backed up by the new laws of quantum physics.

Like most of us, I'm teetering on the cusp of the

new paradigm, and, although I believe in the concept of oneness, I neither *know* it nor *experience* it on a regular basis. One technique I use to help myself move beyond the belief in separateness is visualizing my energy dancing and mingling with both animate and inanimate others, like energy soup. I also remind myself when I meet people going through my day, "I and this person are one" like Christ said of himself and his father. I'm not sure how much progress I'm making, but I do feel more tolerant and connected much of the time. I'm going to keep trying, because oneness is the essence of spiritual love.

I and my sister and brother are one.

Love is essence.

Practicing Beginner's Mind

. . . .

I FIND THE BUDDHIST CONCEPT OF BEGINNER'S mind incredibly refreshing. As adults, we've spent so much time and energy filling our minds with information that they begin to resemble cluttered attics, so glutted with stuff that we can hardly move through them, let alone find what we're looking for. The idea of beginner's mind is to empty, not fill, in order to be ready for anything and open to everything. It's about going back to a time where we knew nothing and therefore took nothing for granted.

It's actually very relaxing to practice beginner's mind. For example, before I was to give a talk to a large group that had labeled me an "expert on relationships," I was anxiety-ridden to the point of sleeplessness. To make matters worse, the "expert" and her husband were not on the best of terms right then. (Don't you hate it when that happens?) I was afraid I wouldn't remember all that I knew, that somehow the audience would know that Gene and I were in a hard place, and that I would embarrass myself, my hosts, and the planet. You know, the usual.

Thankfully, just before I was supposed to leave for the talk, I ran across a quote by Suzuki Roshi that said, "In the beginner's mind there are many possibilities; in the expert's mind there are few." Quick as a wink I dropped the "expert" label and gave the talk as a sister pilgrim on the sometimes rocky path of relationships. My relaxed attitude seemed to translate to the audience because we had a great time.

Anxiety slams the door shut on our mind's attic, whereas beginner's mind not only keeps our attic door open but opens the door to the attic of intuition, which is a vast storehouse of wisdom and joy.

Just for the fun of it, put the book down and look at your surroundings with new eyes. Really see the objects or vistas. Explore your space with the openness of a curious child. Fill yourself with the wonder of beginner's mind.

I practice the art of beginner's mind.

I am open to many possibilities.

Taking the Helm

. . . .

SPIRITUAL GROWTH LIES BEYOND BLAME, FOR blame casts out love and keeps us locked in the childish victimized action of finger pointing. That's why our spirits and souls remain immobile, undeveloped, and thwarted in direct proportion to the amount of blame we harbor.

Since chronic, congealed blame dwarfs and deforms our spiritual development, one of our major life-tasks is to heal, transform, and let go of any blaming energy that we harbor toward ourselves or others. Dropping blame means not *assigning* responsibility to others for our lives, feelings, actions, and words but *assuming* it ourselves.

By taking responsibility, I'm talking about choosing how we *respond* in all situations and assessing our part in creating them or allowing them to happen. I am *not* talking about blaming ourselves by thinking something like, "I have cancer. What horrible thing have I done to deserve this?" But rather, "I have cancer. What emotions or lifestyle choices may have created a vulnerability to it, and what can I do now to change that? How can this situation polish my spirit?"

I believe that we're not helpless in the face of a random world, but that in some unfathomable way our souls have agreed to learn lessons provided by many of the circumstances we face. Assuming responsibility frees us by putting us at the helm of our lives, in charge of mapping out the routes to take on our physical and spiritual journey.

I was talking to Laurel, a wonderfully wise young woman, about the concept of taking responsibility even in difficult situations, and she said something I'll never forget. "Well," she chuckled, "the way I look at it is that, in the In-Between-Lives Lounge, I went to the registration table and said, 'I'll take everything you've got!' So, I'm going to learn from it."

We can lovingly take the helm of our lives, chart our own course, and learn from even treacherous waters. Gently ask yourself if you are sailing in uncharted waters right now. If so, what might you learn by taking the helm and turning in a new direction?

All situations can polish my spirit.

I take responsibility—not blame—for my life.

Caring for Grandmother Earth

. . . .

To indigenous people, Earth is a living being.
Among the Lakota we call Earth our grandmother,
and you do not rape your grandmother. Because
she is the mother of all living beings, you are related
to everything that lives—every blade of grass,
every pine needle, every grain of sand. Even the
rocks have life. Since you rely on all this life for
your sustenance, you have to be respectful.

—Russell Means, Arapaho Activist

AS WOMEN OF SPIRIT, ONE OF THE MOST URGENT
responsibilities we have is to become respectful cit-
izens of Grandmother Earth, not merely consumers
or conquerors, and to teach others to do the same.
Grandmother Earth is our sustainer and inspiration.
She not only provides a home and sustenance, but
her measureless beauty opens a thousand windows
to show us God. Her vast mountains remind us of
the endless peaks of our own courage, the fathom-
less depths of her seas reflect our own enigmatic
and unplumbed treasures, and the endless span of
her ever-changing sky invites our spirits to soar on
the wings of eagles. Next to life itself, Grandmother Earth is God's most precious gift, and it is
our sacred responsibility to cherish her so that our

beloved children will inherit her riches

Today, in reality or in your mind's eye, go to a place on the breast of Grandmother Earth where you feel her power and are inspired by her beauty. Make yourself comfortable and invite the wonder of her priceless and countless gifts to permeate your heart and soul. Ask her what she desires from and of you. Listen for her voice in the wind and from the depths of your heart.

I love and respect Grandmother Earth.
I nourish the earth as she nourishes me.

Slowing the Merry-Go-Round

IF YOUR LIFE NO LONGER FEELS MERRY BUT, in fact, seems more like a perpetual "harried-go-round," then perhaps you are out of sync with the cycles of nature, which are leisurely and rather slow. Sister Moon uses a full month to wax and wane. Flowers bud and bloom slowly. Babies take nine months to fully develop, and we spend an entire lifetime maturing and growing old. But we, goaded by unreasonable internal and external demands, regularly speed our merry-go-round up until it's hard to hang on to our good humor, let alone fill up our spirits.

To have the energy for spiritual growth, we have a sacred responsibility to discern how fast we want our merry-go-round to go. Of course the desired pace will change periodically depending on circumstances, and that is great as long as we have a choice about the velocity of our lives. There will be times when we want to walk in the race of life rather than run. It's easier on our knees, it allows us to see the scenery, and it leaves us enough breath to talk to a friend and enough quiet to hear our own intuitive wisdom. At other times, an all-out run may be exhilarating and will invigorate our hearts, souls, and minds. It's our choice. We just have to make sure that we are choosing our own pace.

With your eyes gently closed, invite the image of a carousel to appear in your mind. Leisurely climb aboard and feel it as it begins to move. How do you like this merry-go-round? Is it circling at a speed that is comfortable for you? Do you like the horse you are on? Is the seat comfortable?

You are the director of your visual picture. Create the ideal carousel, traveling at a satisfactory speed, and then decide how you might want to re-create that rhythm in your day.

I choose the pace that is right for me today.

I match my life to my unique rhythm.

Actualizing Our Vision

....

NO MATTER WHAT OUR LIFE HAS BEEN LIKE UP to this point, it is never too late to be who we are meant to be. Each of us arrives in this life with special talents, aptitudes, and dreams, which we add to, augment, and refine as we mature. These aspirations and yearnings are the visions of our souls, the blueprints of our very being. It is our sacred assignment to actualize our personal visions as best we can, both for our own fulfillment, and as gifts to the planet and humankind. If we sacrifice our dreams or denigrate our gifts out of fear or as a concession to others' desires, we set ourselves up for a life of disappointment and resentment.

Noted scholar Joseph Campbell succintly summed up the consequences of giving up our vision when he said, *"Hell is living someone else's life."* When I first heard that, I was in hell, having given up all my dreams and turning myself inside out in hopes of saving my first marriage. It didn't work.

Although living someone else's life and burning our own dreams and talents on the pyres of fear or obligation may sometimes appear to be succeeding, it never does on the soul level. At the level of Essence, we are being called to be a unique prism through which the Divine can be reflected. In response, every fiber of our being is magnetically drawn toward becoming who we were meant to be. Anything less is hell for our spirit.

Living our own life does not make us selfish and self-centered. Quite the contrary. When we actualize our vision, we become *centered* in our hearts and connected to our spirits, which naturally makes us more loving and less selfish.

What are your special gifts and talents? Do you feel comfortable about how you are expressing them? If so, great. If not, what one small step can you take today or tomorrow to actualize your unique vision?

Each day I become more aware of my vision for myself and my life.

I deserve to live my own life.

Making Peace with Risk

RISK IS A FOUR-LETTER WORD. BUT THEN, SO ARE
live, life, love, and easy. Almost everything has an
element of risk involved, and it's perfectly natural
to be wary of risk. It's even okay to be terrified
occasionally, but terror needs to be accepted as
something to *work through*, not used as a stop sign.

If fear of risk does stop you from living the way
you would like, please find help through therapy or
a support group. There are times when we need
someone else to hold the light for us while we ven-
ture into the dark cellars of our subconscious to
ferret out fear.

A therapist friend of mine took the risk of seeing
very disturbed clients and, when one committed
suicide, every therapist's nightmare came true—
the family sued her. The "justice" system activated
every shred of fear she had cowering in her cellar,
so she escaped to the beach to try and pull herself
together. The shark's teeth sprinkled along the
water's edge gave my friend an idea. At all subse-
quent court hearings she carried shark's teeth in her
pocket. Fingering them while in the presence of
the attorneys helped remind her that she, too, carried some shark energy and could keep herself safe
by not being intimidated by the court process and
by setting acceptable parameters for herself. It was

difficult to make peace with the risks of private practice, but she continued working and is a much stronger person because of the experience.

In order to really expand our spiritual wings, we need to make peace with risk, transform fear, and create a deep sense of security within our hearts. A helpful gift we can give others as we go through our own process is to pray that our efforts are for them as well as ourselves. Asking that our work reach out to benefit the world gives us a sense of purpose and may even level out bumpy roads for others in ways we can't comprehend.

I accept risk as a part of life.
I keep myself as safe and secure as I can.

Gathering in Circles

. . . .

WOMEN EVERYWHERE ARE GATHERING AT THE
spring-fed wells of Spirit to share their hearts and
join hands as they move toward more completely
expressing their boundless love, magnificent wisdom, and compassionate intuition. To these limit-
less wells, each of us carries her *own* container.
Each of us fills her *own* jar. And each of us is also
called to walk with her sisters along the way providing support, guidance, encouragement, inspiration, and love.

The best we have to give is ourselves. Each time
we gather in a sisterly circle that calls forth our
best, a new pattern is stitched into the fabric of the
Spirit-quilt that we are fashioning together, and we
are warmed and protected in its folds. One
women's group I know of that has met for three
years is committed to completing what the members call their "no more guilt quilt." Collectively
and individually they help each other get the guilt-
monkey off their backs.

Do you have a circle of women who cherish
your hopes, are kind to your dreams, and recognize your uniqueness? Is there a safe place where
your spirit is ennobled and you see yourself reflected in the eyes of love and acceptance? It doesn't
matter whether your circle is small or vast. The

important thing is that you are lovingly valued no matter how you feel or what you do, and also that you feel gently challenged to grow your soul. If you don't currently have such a circle, I encourage you to create one.

An ennobling and comforting circle is also as near as your wise imagination. Close your eyes and allow yourself to effortlessly drift into a relaxed state. Visualize yourself surrounded by others who care deeply for you. Sink into their collective arms and accept the love and appreciation they offer. When you're ready, allow love to flow from you to them until you are an integral part of the circle, giving and receiving equally.

I surround myself with people who care for me.

I am safe in a circle of loving friends.

Flowing Through, Not Damming Up

. . . .

IN THE HOLY LAND, THE JORDAN RIVER IS THE source for two lakes. In one, fish are plentiful, wildlife roams its beautiful shores, and thriving villages line its verdant coastline as waters flow through the Lake of Galilee blessing animals, crops, and people alike. Although a recipient of the same in-flow from the Jordan River, the Dead Sea is just that—desolate, deserted. No good for anyone or anything.

The only difference between the two lakes is that one gives, and the other does not. The Lake of Galilee has both an entrance and an outlet allowing the source to flow *through* it, while the Dead Sea receives the waters of the river but doesn't allow them to leave. As a result of hoarding the blessings it receives, the Dead Sea became stagnant and lifeless.

Hearing the above analogy in a sermon, Ann, a client of mine suffering from depression, honestly evaluated where she was on the Dead Sea–Lake of Galilee continuum. Depressed and yet excited by her discovery, she realized that she was like the Dead Sea in terms of giving to others.

Much to her chagrin (and to her credit, I thought), she acknowledged how much she focused on herself and how narrow her world had become.

Courageously, she made a decision to volunteer at a local hospital one day a month. At first, it was only her commitment and a picture of the Dead Sea on her refrigerator that got her out of the house and to the hospital. Eventually, she was volunteering one day a week and looking forward to it. Not surprisingly, having become a blessing to others, she was blessed with a significant lessening of her depression.

The Source, by whatever name you call it, longs to flow into us as a blessing and *through* us as a stream of living water, blessing others. God loves to use us as a floodgate for good. Are you dammed up? Do the waters of love flow through you? Make a promise to yourself today to become like the Lake of Galilee.

I invite divine energy to flow through me.

I enjoy giving to others.

Creating
Spiritual Touchstones

*The best and most beautiful things in the
world cannot be seen or even touched.
They must be felt with the heart.*

—*Helen Keller*

I AGREE WITH HELEN KELLER'S IDEA THAT the best and most beautiful things in the world must be felt with the heart. We can help wonder and beauty permeate our souls by surrounding ourselves with spiritual touchstones that gently nudge our hearts toward remembering the good, true, and beautiful within us and our lives. Remembering feeds our souls.

More often than not, spiritual touchstones are very personal, triggering private memories and beliefs. Cherished objects, rituals, attitudes, habits, and places that center us in our hearts, bring us solace, and help us remember that we are not alone can all be considered spiritual touchstones. A spiritual touchstone may be as momentous as an elaborate wedding ceremony or as simple as the way we greet the day; it may be as valuable as a priceless heirloom or as unpretentious as an acorn. Incorporated into our daily lives, such touchstones can prompt us to be more loving, promote peace of mind, inspire us to a higher purpose, and remind us that we are spiritual beings.

Blessing with Ritual

RITUALS SPEAK THE LANGUAGE OF THE SOUL. During meaningful ritual, divine energy is absorbed not only by our brains but in our hearts and souls as well. Creating and taking part in a ceremony, whether a tiny, solitary blessing or a grand pageant, opens our hearts, connects us with our community and makes us more accessible to ourselves, others, and God.

Profoundly valuable are blessing ceremonies. In them, we intentionally sprinkle Divine grace upon the blessed. Blessing someone or something lifts it into the care and light of God. As we bless, our spirits are also lifted.

Our daily existence is under-blessed; nothing is too minuscule or too magnificent not to benefit from being blessed. We can bless the ill and weary, the food we eat, dead animals along the road, our faces—wrinkles and all—and war-torn countries and the children suffering in them. We can bless anything, even—perhaps, *especially*—our government and political parties. Blessings can be very simple—a silent inward bow, an outstretched hand, the murmuring of a few heartfelt words, a few minutes of deep listening, a sincere thank you. As we bless, we offer our good wishes and make ourselves a conduit for Spirit to flow through.

One of the most moving ceremonies for me was when our family gathered to bless our grandson before he was born. Each of us, in our own way, blessed the forming baby, the mother and her health, and both the mom and dad for the role they were willingly assuming. We told his spirit how much we looked forward to his arrival. After the blessing, our daughter shared that she felt much better, encouraged by our support, and more peaceful about the baby's well-being.

All blessing rituals—private or public—are powerful touchstones that call forth God's love to sanctify both recipient and sender. Take the opportunity today to look through the eyes of Spirit and bestow one or two silent blessings onto people or circumstances that come into your life.

God flows through me as a blessing to myself and others.

God is blessing me now.

Acknowledging Our Abilities

PROUD OF COMPLETING GRADUATE SCHOOL
and finding a good job in her field, Angela recently
congratulated herself by buying a small diamond
ring to complement her wedding ring. Having
been a dedicated stay-at-home mom until now,
gifting herself with something as significant as a
ring was unusual for Angela, but it felt right that
she did it.

The diamond became a literal touchstone for
Angela. When feeling stressed, inadequate, at
odds with a loved one, or in need of a boost, she
developed a private little ritual that restores her
equilibrium: She wears the diamond solitaire
alone, without her wedding ring. The facets in it
symbolize the many aspects of her being, she told
me, and the rainbows of light sparkling from it
help her remember that she sees loving and reflecting the light of God as her highest purpose. And,
very importantly, the single diamond reminds her
of her strength and inspires her to feel good about
who she is and all that she's accomplished. Smiling,
she said, "It just sits there on my finger saying,
'You're good, and you have good to give, so relax.'"

Gently close your eyes for a minute and mentally wander through your mementos. Enjoy them.
Allow them to transport you back in time and

space by the memories they evoke. Is there one that especially symbolizes your unique abilities, talents, and/or gifts? If so, ask your wise subconscious to help you uncover a way that this object can remind you of your special excellence. This is your personal ritual, so nothing is too silly or grandiose. If the right symbol was not available in your mementos, gift yourself with one when you find it.

Spiritual touchstones that help us acknowledge our abilities help to amplify them, thereby allowing us to spread more good to ourselves, others, and Mother Earth, who needs all the good she can get. Actually, we all do!

I am good, and I have good to give.
I am capable, strong, and courageous.

Touching to Remember

WE ARE SENSUOUS BEINGS. WHILE OUR SENSE of touch brings us much pleasure, it's also essential for our emotional well-being. Motherless baby monkeys choose to cuddle with a towel-wrapped wire figure rather than stay around an unwrapped one even though the uncovered "mom" has food by her. We humans are no different than the little monkeys; we need tactile stimulation and solace.

A friend of mine is waging a herculean battle against the cancer invading many areas of her body. Accompanying her to each procedure and all hospital stays is a stuffed lamb given to her by a woman mentor. Gerrie feels less alone and derives physical and emotional comfort from holding her lamb or having him where she can see him. At first, she said it seemed weird to be a grown woman carrying a rather large stuffed toy, but she became increasingly comfortable as doctors, nurses, and friends accepted the lamb as a natural part of her healing.

But the lamb is *not* just a toy for Gerrie, who sees him as a symbol for Christ, the Lamb of God. I wouldn't be surprised if Christ didn't embody that little toy lamb on occasion in order to comfort his pain-ridden child.

As sensual beings, we need touchstones around

us that we can feel in order to nourish our souls and warm our hearts. Such symbols frequently become poignant reminders that we are not alone, but are precious and invaluable, lovable and forever loved by the Divine. As we touch items infused with meaning for us, we can more easily feel ourselves held in the everlasting arms of the Beloved—nurtured, cherished, and comforted.

What touches your heart when you see or feel it? What objects have you gathered around yourself that nourish your soul? We all have them, but oftentimes don't remember to let them soothe us. Just for fun, put one of your symbols in a prominent place as a reminder that you are loved and valued.

I am comforted by meaningful symbols.
I am a loved and lovable child of the Divine.

Swimming in Miracles

EACH DAY WE HAVE THE CHOICE TO SEE WHAT happens as miraculous or ho-hum, and how we choose, dramatically affects our perception of life. The other day miracles were flopping around my feet like little silver grunions at the water's edge. The biggest one happened as I was alone, stewing about how to get home after my bike was sabotaged in a semi-remote area. Just before I dissolved into frustrated tears, a young man happened by who had the strength and know-how to fix my bike. He was only the second person I'd seen all morning.

Being miracle-primed by my knight in shiny bike clothes, I began noticing miracles everywhere. They included a great idea jumping from my heart to the computer screen, totally bypassing my mind, and the top to the teriyaki sauce landing gooey side up when I dropped it.

I started thinking about the reality that even though we may be blind to them, miracles are always swimming around us and are made visible by perceiving life through a lens of wonder and awe. Viewing tiny incidents, synchronicities, and coincidences as minor miracles creates an aura of the miraculous, which lifts our hearts. Henry David Thoreau encouraged us to "associate reverently and

as much as you can, with your loftiest thoughts."
Being miracle-minded invites us into reverence.

Seeing is *creating*. It seems that the more we recognize even the smallest miracle, the more there are to see. When our hearts are tuned toward perceiving miracles, we draw more to us. It's as if the Miracle Makers spread the word, "Hey, everybody! She's finally noticing and appreciating what we've been doing. Let's give 'er a good dousing!"

Swimming in miracles puts us in the flow and allows us to feel the waves of gentle kisses bestowed upon us by a benevolent universe. Create some miracles in your life today by *seeing* the ones that are already joyfully swimming around you.

I notice and celebrate even the tiniest miracle.

My heart is deeply grateful for the miracles sprinkling my days.

Greeting Each Newborn Day

. . . .

WAKING UP IS THE FIRST GIFT THAT WE receive each day. With it, comes the opportunity to set the tone for all of our waking hours. If we usually lament, "Oh, God! It's morning . . ." we can make a big difference in our attitude and energy level by simply changing our greeting to something like, "Thank you, God, for letting me see this morning." When we approach life in this manner, we connect to the wonder of being alive and remember our relationship to the Divine.

If you're already a "lark" instead of a "night owl" and spring out of bed fully awake and enthusiastic, then the following meditation isn't for you, but you may want to read it just to congratulate yourself on mornings well done.

Softly close your eyes and begin to breathe deeply, in through your nose and out through your mouth. As you inhale invite relaxation to flow into your entire body, especially into your brain. Melt into the warmth and comfort of a relaxed body and mind. Absorb the sensation. Compassionately and impersonally, remember how you normally wake up. Without judgment, ask yourself if you are entirely happy with the way you usually greet the day.

If the answer is no, imagine how you'd like to

change your greeting. For instance, what would it be like if you decided to greet each new day with a welcoming smile, just as you would greet a returning old friend? In terms of perspective and language, how could you choose to befriend each virgin day? Slowly, gently visualize yourself in bed right before waking. See yourself, in the perfect, right time and way, awakening to the gift of a pure, new day. Greet it in the fresh way that you imagined. How does that feel?

We create a powerful connection to Spirit by greeting each newborn day with enthusiasm and thankfulness.

This day is a gift from the Divine and I rejoice in it.

When the face in the mirror frowns, I smile back.

Enjoying Several Seconds of Bliss

ALTHOUGH WE MAY HAVE EXTENDED PERIODS of profound joy, most of our truly blissful moments are fleeting. Like sexual orgasms, they are short, but sweetly change us physically, emotionally, and spiritually. We need to gather these blissful moments as we would precious gems and thread them on a memory strand to be lovingly caressed and reverently remembered with gratitude. When used like prayer beads, each memory creates several seconds of bliss for our souls and a rendezvous with the Divine.

Seconds that bathe my spirit in bliss include a short conversation in which I feel deeply understood, a beautiful fox in the driveway, receiving unexpected appreciation from my children, seeing a picture that reminds me of living in Hawaii, being gleefully greeted by my grandson, and a minute in meditation when I feel wholly connected with the Beloved.

Take a little quiet time to think of, or write down, some of *your* blissful moments. When you have a list compiled, gently close your eyes and allow yourself to move into a calm, relaxed state. Settle down comfortably and imagine yourself transported to a fabulous room filled with every conceivable precious and semi-precious gem. In this magical space there are also other treasures that fill your heart with a deep appreciation for their unique qualities.

Leisurely wander among the riches. Choose a strand of some fine, yet strong, material upon which to string your blissful moments. With great care, pick an appropriate symbol for each memory and add it to your strand in exactly the way that pleases you. After you have completed your strand, find a cozy spot where you feel snug and content. With a prayerful attitude caress the touchstones upon your strand. Take the memory of each blissful moment into your heart and feed your soul with its exquisite loveliness. Before returning from this meditative prayer, decide on a place in your home or on your person where you would like your memory strand to abide.

I am thankful for the moments of bliss that bless my life.

I stop often to enjoy several seconds of bliss.

Lifting into the Light

WHILE RELIGION AND MYSTICISM HAVE LONG recognized the power of prayer to affect our energy, attitude, and healing, science is now hopping on the bandwagon. My favorite scientific study was done at Spindrift Institute, where grass seeds were soaked in salt water to keep them from germinating. The seeds were then divided into three groups. The first group was left alone. The second was prayed for by volunteers using directed prayer such as, "Please help these seeds to germinate." The third was the recipient of nondirected prayer that included such statements as, "Thy will be done," or visualizing the seeds whole and perfect and able to germinate if it is the right outworking for them in God's eyes.

Interestingly, none of the seeds from the first group sprouted. And, although some of the ones in the directed prayer group did germinate, *two to four* times as many seeds sprouted when they were prayed for in a nondirective way.

After reading about this study, I decided to place a perpetual prayer candle on my kitchen counter. Beside the candle is a little box in which I place the names of people for whom I want to pray. Before lighting a new candle, I put my hands around it and pray some version of the following: "Mother/Father

God, please infuse this candle with your energy so that each person here will feel the touch of your blessing, the kiss of your compassion, and the solace of your arms." For me, the candle acts as a reminder to lift those named into the light of God for the perfect, right outworking in His/Her eyes.

Our prayers are important and valuable, but it appears that, for the best outcome of all souls concerned, the more nondirective we can be, the better. Realizing how valuable they are, what prayers can you offer today, for yourself and others?

I trust that the Divine and her angels know best.

I lift myself and others into the light of God.

Receiving Solace from the Moon

IN PLAIN VIEW, SHE READILY DISPLAYS HER cycles of illumination and shadow, which are powerful enough to influence vast oceans. Steady, constant, incredibly beautiful, she brings light into the darkness. The moon is our icon, eternally feminine—a celestial mentor, infusing us with the recognition of our own oftentimes shadowy brilliance.

Throughout the centuries, as religions espoused the idea that only the masculine was holy, the power and significance of Sister Moon was progressively downgraded. But a more balanced awareness is emerging and we are realizing that to be whole, holiness must naturally embrace all complementary aspects of being—masculine and feminine, darkness and light, body and spirit, thought and feeling.

As women, we carry the essence of femininity that is symbolized by Sister Moon within the cells of our bodies and the fabric of our souls. Intuitively we can recognize the significance of Luna, the Creator Goddess, and we can invite her to resume her rightful place as our teacher. Once revered and called by the sacred names of "Mother of the Universe," "the Old Woman Who Never Dies," and "The Eternal One," the moon can bring us solace while inspiring us to learn from and respect all of our own natural cycles—the ebbs and flows, ups and downs, and the waxing and waning.

One night after putting her children to bed Judy, a young woman going through a painful divorce, sat on the floor and leaned her forehead on the sliding glass door weeping uncontrollably. As her tears slowed, she felt as if she were being cradled by a loving and tender grandmother. Resting in those gentle arms, a little glimmer of peace began to shine in her heart. "When I opened my eyes, the first thing I saw was the full moon, and I just seemed to know that hers were the arms that held me. Ever since then I've felt a very special kinship with the moon."

As daughters of the moon we, too, are called to bring light into darkness. What tears can you dry today? What gentle arms can you provide for yourself or another?

Waxing and waning
Bringing light into darkness
She smiles her blessing.

Sending Love Darts

· ·

LOVE IS THE SOURCE; FROM IT FLOWS OPEN-hearted trust, service, honor, awe, humor, compassion, commitment, and pristine joy. This sounds esoteric and highfalutin', but it's simply a matter of energy. We all know how energized we feel when love is flowing freely in our lives and, in contrast, how stymied we feel when love is frozen. Why? Because, when love is freely flowing, we are in tune with the energy of our soul-self. When love is blocked we are cut off from it.

The ultimate gift of all relationships is energy—an exorbitant, lavish, luxurious profusion of energy. When flowing, such energy is a creative fountain, a font of well-being from which we can not only revitalize ourselves and others but tackle projects that serve the greater whole.

When we're "in the flow" with God, ourselves, and others, we are energized and have incredible stamina. But if our love-flow is sidetracked or stymied, we feel droopy, cut off, and out of steam. So how do we keep the flow going? One of the simplest and most effective ways is to consciously send little love darts from our hearts toward people we encounter throughout the day—especially the irritating ones.

Love darts are quick, silent blessings to the

recipient—something like, may you be peaceful and happy—and little reminders to ourselves that keep our hearts warm, moist, and fertile. Try it with people whom you're crazy about, and those with whom you have difficulty.

My favorite target is a surly check-out person at the grocery store. I don't know how he feels being pricked by a love dart, but I certainly feel better after sending one than I do when I grouse to myself about how rude he is.

Our commitment to living from the heart and sending positive regard infuses us with the energy of love, and there is no greater or more efficient fuel. Send a quiver of love darts today.

I bless myself with lots of little love darts.

The love of God flows through my heart,
blessing all those whom I encounter.

Being Sensitive to God's Bouquets

IF WE OPEN THE DOOR TO OUR HEART, GOD will throw in a bunch of flowers. Because these sweet bouquets come in myriad forms and are often very subtle, we need to be sensitive to their presence. Learning to open up to receive God's flowers is so important, for they can ease our hearts and become precious reminders of Her caring and concern for us.

God's bouquets often come to us when we need them most, and being able to perceive them is a talent we can cultivate through awareness. Paradoxically, we have a tendency to be very inner-focused and less aware of externals when we are in some sort of pain, so the first step toward seeing God-signs is to actively look for them.

Not long ago I was in the painful place of questioning the meaning and message of my work concerning activating heart energy in relationships. I was still in the loss-of-confidence and lamenting stage, when I found a piece of marble at a sculpting studio—a heart half emerging from a cool white square. A blunt but valuable bouquet from God, and I got the message. Although in need of filing and smoothing, just as my own heart is, the half heart sits on my desk as a reminder to be whole-hearted in my commitment to my work no matter what the consequences or rewards.

Since then, I have stumbled on two more rocks that look like fully formed hearts and a cattail in the form of a heart. The last rock, which had *two* hearts on it, made me laugh in acknowledgment, "Thank you for the vote of confidence! I can sit back down at my computer now."

God's bouquets surround us, but we must be sensitive to their presence in order to enjoy and benefit from them. Give yourself the gift of being on the lookout, for you never know when the heavenly FTD will drop a gift from God into your heart.

I open my eyes to God's blessings.

I am surrounded by reassurance from the Divine.

Cleansing Keepsakes

INTUITIVELY WE KNOW THAT OBJECTS CARRY the energy of those who have owned them. Most of us like to have at least a few keepsakes around us precisely because we can *feel* their energy, which is excellent as long as it is positive. Because they are such storehouses of energy, it's best to keep objects or pictures that carry only positive energy and memories. However, if there is something that you want to keep, but it feels negative to you or brings up painful memories, it can be cleansed and neutralized through prayer and ritual.

Elizabeth was given diaries kept by her grandmother and great-grandmother, neither of whom were grand. Although she wanted to keep the diaries because of their historical significance, Elizabeth felt uncomfortable with them in her home. We created a cleansing ritual for her to do after which she could assess how the books felt to her. First, Elizabeth gave thanks for both women and asked that they be healed and blessed. She then asked Mother Mary to cleanse the diaries, transforming and transmuting the energy in them to energy compatible with the mind of Christ. She evoked her guardian angels to take any stubborn negative energy out of the books and out of her house. Sprinkling the books with a few drops of holy water from Ireland, Elizabeth put them in the light of the sun for a short while.

It seemed to do the trick because Elizabeth is perfectly comfortable with them now and is gleaning a better understanding of why her grandmothers were the way they were through reading them.

Take an intuitive tour through your home and office. Are there objects calling for cleansing because the energy needs transforming and transmuting? You can do it. Simply go to your wise heart and ask to be guided. Whatever works for you is correct. Keepsakes can be wonderful touchstones from which we gain great solace, pleasure, and strength, as long as their energy complements our own.

I have the wisdom and right to cleanse any object.

I trust my feelings and intuitions.

Savoring Our Souls

BECAUSE THE DEMANDS OF DAY-TO-DAY LIFE have a way of dulling our spirits and cutting us off from our hearts, it's essential that we find ways to reinstate solitude into our lives and, through it, experience the beauty of heart and soul. One day, while suffering from solitude starvation, I ran across a poem in which the poet talked about wandering alone through his house savoring and kissing the fallen crumbs of his soul.

I smiled as I read the poem because it validated the feelings I often have while home alone. I wander—touching, appreciating, remembering, singing, gathering, and kissing the fallen crumbs of my soul. Very often this is the time that I choose to change the symbols in the miniature Zen sand garden given to me by my son. A simple task, taking only a few minutes at the most, but nonetheless a richly replenishing ritual in which I savor my soul.

If your soul has been dropping a trail of crumbs as it accompanies your body through its days, how would you like to savor and nourish it? Can you arrange for some solitary time at home in which you sweep up and kiss your soul crumbs?

Gently close your eyes and imagine a time in your own home when you are blessed by the renewal of solitude. Cherish it. Wander or sit quietly. Give

yourself the gift of enjoying the solitude in ways
that warm your heart, fill your spirit, and revitalize
your soul.

It is a sacred assignment to rescue the crumbs of
our souls that have been kicked under the table by
too much activity and too little aloneness, and to
collect and kiss them "all better."

I need and deserve time alone.

I am adept at balancing time alone and time with others.

Awakening to Wisdom

When sleeping women wake,
mountains move.

—Chinese proverb

WE ARE ALL AWARE THAT THERE ARE many mountains in need of moving. Mountains of ignorance and intolerance need to be transformed into peaks of understanding and acceptance, mountains of materialism must be lowered, and mountains of inequality must be transformed into partnership, respect, and egalitarianism.

We who bear the feminine qualities of compassion, intuition, and inclusion are called to awaken to our own prodigious wisdom and to move the mountains that block our paths and obliterate both Brother Sun and Sister Moon. Through our wisdom, we can fashion a powerfully creative and joyful life for ourselves and institute changes that will build a better world for our children and their children's children.

As with everything else, awakening to wisdom begins with ourselves as we realize that each of us is a creation of the Divine and therefore an expression and fulfillment of Divine purpose. As they say in Hawaii, "God don't make junk!" Far from being junk, at the center of our souls, we are innately, inherently, and incredibly wise. When we awaken to and act from our wisdom, mountains will move and the Divine will smile with satisfaction.

Becoming a Wisdom Gatherer

THE ANCIENT TERMINOLOGY FOR THE STAGES of a woman's life—Maiden, Mother, and Crone—needs to be expanded now that women are living much longer. Inserted between Mother and Crone is a necessary and fulfilling stage that I call Wisdom Gatherer.

Of course we gather wisdom all through our lives, but in keeping with the saying, "Given enough time and nourishment, sage will replace wild oats in the garden of life," midlife usually provides more opportunities for cultivating sage-filled wisdom than do the previous stages of Maiden or Mother. In the first, we are rightly cultivating ourselves; who we are, what we believe, and what values we hold dear. As Mothers, we often concentrate more on cultivating and nourishing the lives of others; if not children, then career, mate, or personal dreams.

The Wisdom Gatherer period is often the time when women wake and mountains begin to move. In this phase, our souls invite us to mature in spirit, acknowledge and build on our unique gifts and talents, and glean wisdom from our experiences through thoughtful contemplation. Ideally, as Wisdom Gatherers, we take measure of ourselves—gently, realistically, and with honor—and in so doing, we see ourselves as highly capable and truly miraculous beings. During this period we cull all that we have learned and all that we intuitively know. Such introspection ushers us through the age of Wisdom Gatherer toward the eventual crown of Cronedom, or Eldership.

No matter what age you are, you can gather wisdom. Imagine yourself carrying a beautiful, hand-woven basket as you move through the garden of life. Each circumstance, experience, and relationship has the potential for becoming a stunning blossom of compassion or a fragrant bundle of sage.

Think about the wisdom that you have gathered thus far. Give yourself credit for the ways in which you have grown and blossomed and for the ways that you've helped others grow. Appreciating ourselves each day gives us the courage to gather the seeds and stomp through the fertilizer, both of which are necessary to keep our garden of wisdom growing.

Each experience has within it a seed of wisdom.

I gather wisdom as I go through life.

Tending the Creative Fires

. . . .

OF ALL THE QUALITIES IN OUR BEING, THE ONE
that is the most Godlike is creativity. Creativity is
wisdom in action—a powerful, intangible, and
deeply spiritual birthright.

We are born from the Creator to create, and,
therefore, are fired by a primal desire to express our
unique and individual creativity. Our universe is
continually creating itself, and our bodies are in a
constant state of re-creation. As an example: skin,
scrapped, seared, or sliced immediately begins to
create new skin. We take it for granted. Yet, such
re-creation is an unconscious, instinctual miracle.

Consciously, our compulsion to create is no less
compelling. Although our creative fires may have
been dampened from our life circumstances up to
this point, they are waiting, smoldering for us to
rebuild them. Because creativity and wisdom are
fraternal twins, tending our creative fires is a wonderful way to ignite and awaken to our wisdom.
"Why should we all use our creative powers . . . ?"
asks writer Brenda Ueland. "Because there is nothing that makes people so generous, joyful, lively,
bold and compassionate, so indifferent to fighting
and the accumulation of objects and money."
Sounds Godlike to me.

With quiet excitement, close your eyes and

begin to deepen your breath. As you inhale say, "I am," and as you exhale say, "creative." I am . . . creative. I am . . . creative. Relaxing softly into the center of your being, visualize yourself tending a beautiful, vibrant, but in-control fire. Enjoy it in whatever ways feel good to you. This is your creative fire. What sparks need fanning? What new logs are yearning to be added? What passionate part of this fire needs to express itself more freely in order to feed your soul?

We are created in God's image. Would that not mean that one of our most natural gifts is to express creativity? Give yourself the gift of kindling the flames of your creativity, the light of which will illuminate your wisdom.

My creativity is wise, wonderful, and fun.

I make time to express my creativity.

Mining the Gold of Dreams

DREAMS ARE A DIRECT PIPELINE FROM THE Divine. Although dreams are sometimes purely entertainment, very often they are symbolic wisdom lessons graphically showing us what is right and wrong in our lives and offering previews of coming attractions as well as hints about pitfalls that may dot our path. Reoccurring dreams are especially important wisdom teachers imploring us to pay attention.

Dreams may be the Spirit's easiest channel through which to communicate with us, but they are also the most elusive. Who hasn't awakened from a profoundly moving dream only to have its substance immediately quick-silver out of reach? If remembering dreams doesn't come naturally to us, we can train ourselves to become good at it.

Teaching ourselves to seize evasive dream messages is a two-layered process. On the spiritual/mind level, we need to set our intention and instruct our conscious mind to remember our dreams clearly. Before going to sleep, it's important to reaffirm the intention to remember and consciously welcome dreams as wisdom tools. We can then ask our higher selves or guardian angels for help.

On a physical level, it's usually a must to have

paper and pen beside the bed to write down at least a memory jog, but *before moving even a fraction* immediately replay the dream. Movement shakes many dreams right out of awareness. Title your dreams and journal with and about them. Remember, you are your own best expert for interpreting your dreams.

Unless we are naturally adept at it, dream harvesting takes consistent practice and commitment. For many people, it's easy at times and almost impossible at others. Congratulate yourself for recalling even tiny fragments or remembering the barest hint of a feeling evoked by a dream. Becoming aware of our dreams creates the opportunity for nightly showers of Divine influence.

I effortlessly remember my dreams.

My dreams are a source of pleasure, affirmation, and instruction.

Living Our Dreams

THE HEIGHT OF WISDOM IS BEING WILLING TO live out our dreams, for they are urgings from our souls encouraging us to progress in the way that is right for us.

If we have lost track of our aspirations, those we had in childhood were often the wisdom of our souls telling us what our hearts desired. As children we were still close to the Source and, therefore, our dreams were very important signposts. But a child intuitively knows whether her aspirations will be heard or denied by her family, and, if ours were denied, we may have learned to ignore them and live another person's dreams or let dreams go altogether.

Irene de Castillejo, in her book *Knowing Woman*, underscored the importance of living our own dreams: "Life insists on being lived, and anything that belongs to life which is allowed to lie dormant has to be lived by someone else. If we do not accept our shadow we force our children to carry the burden of our undeveloped capacities. They may become mediocre scientists or artists because we denied our own talents."

Right now, very gently, but with total honesty, ask yourself, "Am I trying to live out an unexpressed dream of a parent or other person in my life?" "Is a child of *mine* living out a talent that I have not developed?" and "Am I letting dreams lie dormant?"

If you suspect the answers may be yes or if you're unsure about what your own dreams are, close your eyes for a moment and allow your mind to roam back to the years when you were a kid. What did you long to be when you grew up? Who were your heroines? What books or television programs did you relate to? What dreams have you given up as impractical? Please listen to the soul-call of your dreams and creatively find ways to bring them to fruition.

I have the wisdom to bring my dreams
and aspirations to fruition.

Each day my dreams.become clearer to me.

Finding Work with Heart

AT SOME DEEP LEVEL, EVERY ONE OF US WANTS to be of service to the world through meaningful work. But often finding that work is elusive, and we wander from job to job or stay in a dead-end job, never quite connecting to our soul's purpose.

The issue was front and center for me during my divorce. Because my self-esteem had to reach up to touch bottom at the time and I had only worked spasmodically during my marriage, I had no idea what I could do. However, in the midst of my terror, constantly and doggedly—without even a glimmer of faith on many occasions—I affirmed, "Each day I become clearer as to the work that is right for me in God's eyes." and prayed, "Help me have the clarity to see and hear the message, and the guts to follow through with it!"

There was never a bolt of lightning scorching "Thou shalt be a therapist," onto my brain, which was a good thing because I probably would have replied in horror, "I can't possibly be a therapist, but I sure do need one!" No, my prayers were answered one tiny little nudge at a time, baby-steps that I could garner the courage to take.

In order for you to get a sense of how to find meaningful soul-work, ask yourself the following questions: What do you find meaningful in life?

What does your heart long to contribute to the world? What services are you equipped to provide? Who needs them? and, Do you want to give them? If you won a big lotto drawing, what would you do? Would that feel meaningful to you in the long run?

Although it is sometimes difficult, please trust that the wisdom within you *knows* what work is right for you. Today, ask God, your angels, and your soul-Self for help in arranging the perfect, right work for you.

*Each day I become clearer as to the work
that is right for me in God's eyes.*

I open myself to finding and accepting work with heart.

Clearing Away the Cobwebs

. . . .

MY DAD USED TO SAY, "I'M GOING OUT TO BLOW the stink off and clear away the cobwebs," when leaving the house for a walk or bike ride. I don't know about the stink, but it's a well-known fact that exercise helps our bodies work more efficiently and clears the cobwebs from our minds. A friend of mine who works with elderly people says it is amazing how just a little bit of exercise helps her residents to sleep better, feel less depressed, and sharpen their mental acumen. Rumor has it that some have also rekindled their interest in romance.

It's especially wonderful when we can exercise outdoors where there is the opportunity to immerse ourselves in beauty and greet other people. Actually, we might get ourselves moving better if we changed the idea of "exercise" to something with less drudgery attached to it such as, "I'm going out to say 'hi' to Mother Nature," or "I'll be playing on the treadmill for the next twenty minutes." No matter what form of movement we choose, it needs to have an element of fun, adventure, or pleasure attached. It's okay if the pleasure is as subtle as feeling a little more alert. That's great. That's clearing away cobwebs.

If you already exercise and enjoy it, wonderful. If you don't, what can you do today to move your body just a little? Put on some music and dance a step or two? Walk down the stairs when going to lunch? Stretch the muscles in your neck and arms? Bodies, as well as minds and hearts, need to be stretched regularly.

In order to clear away the cobwebs, ener-gize ourselves, and better access the wisdom of our intuition and our intellect, we need to give ourselves the gift of daily, enjoyable movement. Our bodies, hearts, and minds will all be thankful.

I exercise and enjoy it.

I love my body, heart, and mind, and I exercise them daily.

Freeing Inner Elders

EACH OF US HAS WITHIN HER EMISSARIES OF Light, inner elders who need to be recognized and claimed as we awaken to our wisdom. We have been so brainwashed by puritanical facets of our culture into believing that we are innately sinful and shameful beings that we tend to negate, ignore, and distrust our light-filled, divine selves. But don't be surprised if you meet a mystic, priestess, artist, philosopher, or gathering of wise elders as you explore the depths and heights of your inner self.

The Light is within us. We are asked to know ourselves, sunbeams and shadows alike, and, through love and acceptance, transform our shadow material, liberating its life force to become a source of light, vitality, and power. The diamond of our being sparkles more brilliantly when all facets are turned toward the light.

Our inner elders retain their innocence and divinity no matter what wounds we may have sustained in the school of life. As reflections of the Beloved's fire, Emissaries of Light are eternally willing to illuminate our paths. Opening to them and accepting their reality invites their wisdom to guide us. When set free, the elders of our souls can guide us in our quest for reunion with God.

Close your eyes and gently encourage your

body to relax and your mind to quiet. Breathe deeply in through your nose and out through your mouth. Sink ever more deeply into the soft silence. As you feel ready, see or sense yourself in the midst of a gathering of wise elders. One or two of them may be clearer to you than the others. If you don't feel blessed by their presence, allow them to fade and invite in others with whom you feel absolutely loved. Immerse yourself in their love, honoring the fact that these elders are an integral part of your vast storehouse of wisdom.

I have within me a vast storehouse of wisdom.

I and my Emissaries of Light dance joyfully with the Beloved.

Integrating the Black Madonna

STATUES AND OTHER IMAGES OF THE BLACK Madonna abound in the lowliest chapels and most grandiose cathedrals in Europe. These dark relics represent woman's essential, but much maligned shadow aspects—the powerful, earthy, humorous, lusty, fertile, disciplined, and outspoken qualities that were stripped from the Virgin Mary in the first few centuries A.D. Mary was not always portrayed as a meek, long-suffering, and submissive woman, however. To many who trust their intuition, Mary was, and is, viewed as the feminine aspect of God, a powerful, compassionate, and wise deity.

The Black Madonna and the Virgin Mary represent two halves of a whole Divine Feminine, a sacred partnership. Actually, in our universe, everything is complemented by an opposite. For instance, male and female must combine to reproduce, and the synergy of dark and light creates night and day. But a more alchemical symbol for the synergistic combination of opposites is the yin-yang sign. In it, light and shadow fit together in a graceful curve—each containing a circle of the other within itself. Intertwined, they form a perfect circle, which is the universal symbol of wholeness and infinity.

We, too, carry the same complementary opposites represented by the Black Madonna and the Virgin Mary. In order to form a balanced whole, we need to integrate both within our psyches and spirits. Do you acknowledge the powerful qualities of the Black Madonna within you? Do you allow the soft gentleness of the Virgin to express through you? Working on integrating the power of the Black Madonna is one of my lifelong tasks, and one that I didn't make much progress with until I was over fifty.

Individually and worldwide, we need both the earthy and the ethereal, the power and the compassion, and the dark and the light. We can integrate and act from both.

I accept all aspects of myself.

I constructively express both the light and dark within me.

Gleaning from Mistakes
and Failures

. . . .

AS AMERICAN POLITICAL ACTIVIST DOROTHY
McCall says, "One cannot have wisdom without living life." Because we are human and fallible, throwing ourselves enthusiastically into the business of
living naturally means that we will stumble and fall
occasionally. Real people living real lives make mistakes and experience failure. It's what we do with
our mistakes and failures that makes the difference.
If we get caught in the perfectionist's lament of "If I
can't do it perfectly, I won't do it at all," or if we
berate ourselves to such an extent that we're too
frightened to try new things, we're not gleaning the
valuable lessons inherent in our setbacks.

If, on the other hand, we realize that perfection
does not tolerate mistakes whereas excellence incorporates mistakes and learns from them, we can toss
perfectionism in the garbage and glean value from
failure. We're here to learn. With just a small tilt in
attitude, moving from the need to appear perfect to
the willingness to see mistakes as opportunities for
great growth and learning, we can make our lives
so much more serene and fun.

Deciding to commit to excellence instead of
perfection, we can welcome our mistakes with a

lighter attitude and let them shed light on our progressive path toward wisdom. We can "lighten up!" as one of the most profound spiritual colloquialisms of our day encourages.

Write a list of any persistent shoulds and oughts that keep at least one of your feet solidly perched on the precarious platform of perfectionism. Write another, more life-friendly message, giving yourself permission to *acquire* skills and *learn* lessons through trial and error. Symbolically, or literally, toss your first list in the garbage.

On the sea of life, we're all in the same boat, and very few of us arrived automatically knowing how to row or set the sails.

I gently encourage myself to learn from mistakes and failures.

I try to "lighten up" my heavy attitudes.

Emulating the Willow

. . . .

*That the yielding conquers the resistant and the soft
conquers the hard is a fact known to all [wo]men,
yet utilized by none.*
—Lao Tzu

SEATED BENEATH A LARGE WILLOW TREE
watching its leafy fingertips lightly brushing the
surface of a small pond, I had a compelling desire
to become her student. Silently, I implored, "Please
teach me to be unaffected by life's storms through
wisely yielding to their turbulence. Show me, dear
sister, how to conquer the hard attitudes of some
people by softening my own. Help me stop resisting philosophies and opinions that I find righteous
and intolerable and, instead, shine light and impersonal love upon their bearers. Help me dance with
the winds of Spirit and not stiffen in my own beliefs
of how things should be evolving."

How can we be a willow but not a wimp? So
often resistance appears to be the only way, and
conquering through soft yielding seems merely a
fantasy. We can learn the wisdom of the willow and
open our hearts to its counsel. For a few moments
give yourself the joy of imagining that you are a
beautiful, strong, and flexible willow tree.

Visualize an exquisite setting for yourself as the

most feminine of trees. Feel your roots firmly implanted on the breast of Mother Earth, and, if you'd like, get up and allow your body to sway as if the wind were playing (or raging) through your graceful branches. Soak in the sense of willowness. Flexibility, strength, beauty, resilience, durability, grace, acceptance, wisdom—all of these qualities are hers. All are also yours. Where in your life do you need to emulate the willow more than you currently are? From the depths of your wise feminine heart, can you encourage yourself to become more willowlike in attitude and action?

I am both flexible and strong.
I easily dance with the winds of life.

Being in the Flow

....

ARTISTS OF ALL KINDS—WRITERS, PAINTERS, counselors, musicians, parents, lovers, sculptors, teachers, entrepreneurs—often speak of their very creative times as "being in the flow." While in the flow, life functions like a beautifully choreographed ice skating routine. Effortlessly, we glide through a project or conversation as if lubricated by angel oil. It feels great!

While some of those times are gifts of grace, more often we have primed the pump by having positive attitudes as well as following through with our commitment to sit at the computer, teach the class, do one more parental chore, or quiet our mind through solitude, meditation, and introspection. Mentally and physically, we've prepared ourselves and made a commitment. As a result, the magical "flow" answers our call.

Becoming increasingly gentle with who we really are will help us remain in the flow of our lives rather than continually thrashing exhaustedlyagainst the current. We grow into the wisdom of going with the flow by accepting and trusting our own excellence and the benevolence of the Divine.

Patty, a wise friend of mine, once told me that her most profound workshop experience came from a group singing "Row, row, row your boat gently down the stream" for over a half hour. At first, she groused to herself what a colossal waste of time and money this was, but she finally began to flow along *with* the current of the experience and *got*, at a deep gut level, how much—and not at all merrily—she tried to swim against the current in her daily life. For Patty, that little ditty became a mantra that helped her learn to live in the flow of life.

Having the wisdom to tap into the artistry of life by rowing our boats gently *down* the stream brings increasing freedom to our spirits and solace to our souls.

I row gently and merrily downstream.

I have the wisdom and courage to trust both God and myself.

Planting Where We Are Blooming

WE'VE ALL HEARD THE WONDERFUL LITTLE aphorism, "Bloom where you are planted." However, the opposite is equally true. We have already planted seeds of insight, compassion, and inspiration where we are blooming. In precisely the areas where we naturally excel or have diligently worked to be able to shine, others are benefiting from the fruits and flowers of our accrued wisdom.

For example, Bobbie, who is a wonderful parent, has written an equally wonderful parenting book; Bonnie, who has absolutely fallen in love with grandparenting, gives classes to grandparents on the art of mentoring grandchildren; and Carolyn, who has always loved being around elderly people, is now shepherding her mother toward heaven's gate. Each of these women is planting a garden for others where they, themselves, already bloom. In Carolyn's case, not only is she planting seeds for a grace-filled death for her mom, but she is sowing the seeds of her own future in which she hopes to work in the field of gerontology.

Where are you already blooming? In what field do you flower exceptionally well? Where does your wisdom shine brightly?

Take a few moments now to meditate on ways and places in which you are in full bloom. If you find it difficult to be aware of your own flowering, imagine that your dearest friend is telling you how she perceives your blooming. What seeds of wisdom are you now planting, and what others can you plant in order to beautify the garden of life?

Be generously honest, for one of the most significant things women can do is awaken to, welcome, and accept their own wisdom. Only then can we plant seeds of service and share our fertile wisdom and compassion for the benefit of those whom we love and those whom we may never meet.

I flower beautifully in the area of _____ .

I share my wisdom and love with others.

Enrolling in
Saint's School

*One thing that comes out of myths is that
at the bottom of the abyss comes the voice
of salvation. The black moment is the
moment when the real message of
transformation is going to come.
At the darkest moment comes the light.*

—Joseph Campbell

I ONCE HEARD STEPHEN LEVINE TELL A NEWLY diagnosed ALS patient that, through his illness, he had been enrolled in Saint's School. We all have the option of enrolling in Saint's School when called upon to grapple with trauma, pain, and death. It's an excellent choice to view crises and afflictions as a school in which we can hone our souls, for how we handle the lessons life presents determines whether we eventually attain the serenity and peace of mind of a saint or endure the demons of agitation, bitterness, resentment, and depression.

Crisis is a part of the human cycle. We ascend, flourish, bear fruit, and then, seemingly as an answer to the law of gravity, we arch, hit a plateau, descend, and die to the part of us wounded in crisis. Because feminine energy is deeply aware of and in tune with cycles, crisis is best handled by the Sacred Feminine within us. She, in her wisdom, knows that crisis is followed by rebirth. When a part of us—an old pattern, an expectation, a role, a loved one—is washed away in the alchemy of crisis, new parts of our being and new possibilities for our lives are conceived and born. Trauma and transformation walk hand in hand. In joy, we are blessed, and, through sorrow we are given the opportunity to become a blessing.

Kissing the Darkness

As human beings, we are all enrolled in Saint's School at some time or other. There are daily lessons to learn and daily losses to release, but many of us seem to study these assignments most often under the blanket of night.

Night blurs the revealing corners of day, obscuring the familiar pegs upon which we hang our facades. Stoic masks dissolve as our most fundamental fears parade in the darkness. Stripped of day's bright distractions, night finds us alone, its black mirror reflecting and magnifying our deepest concerns. In the profound shadows of night, the apocalypse horses of isolation and despair may try to drag us from our daytime strength into a pit of relentless anxiety and self-pity.

However, we can choose, instead, to descend to the heights of our soul by kissing the darkness hello. We can embrace the fertility of "night school" by blessing our pain while exploring the insights that it offers. Kissing the darkness invites it to reveal its mysteries to us, but kicking the darkness away creates unresolved issues, which fester into chronic pain and limitations. For, as we all know but must relearn over and over, resistance only magnifies pain

If you are currently taking night classes in Saint's

School, gently prepare by making a plan to comfort yourself when sleep will not come and darkness is your only company. Perhaps a cup of your favorite tea ready to be brewed, candles waiting to be lighted, a journal and pen at the ready, and a cozy afghan will help give you the courage to glean the wisdom offered by your present experience.

When, through crisis, loss, or chaos, we rotate away from the light of our being, much like the earth rotates away from the sun at night, it's best to kiss the darkness as we fall under its shadow and open to our pain and meet it in the depths of our wise hearts. Doing so ensures the dawn of a new day.

I have the courage to explore the lessons revealed in the fertile darkness.

I accept both light and dark in my life.

Being Responsible to *Our Crises, Not for Them*

. . . .

ACCEPTANCE OF SUFFERING CHANGES CRISIS from tormentor to teacher. True acceptance, with an eye and ear toward what we can learn from a crisis, has nothing to do with being a helpless victim of circumstances. Rarely, if ever, is there anything to gain from viewing ourselves as a victim, but there is everything to gain from seeing ourselves as a student in each situation.

Some popular philosophies believe that we create everything that happens to us, and to a certain extent that's probably true, but surely Life and Spirit are so mysterious and unfathomable that it's a little grandiose of us to believe that we know exactly what creates what.

In reality, we can't always choose what will happen to us, or even *in* us, but we are free to choose how we will respond. We *can* choose to learn from everything that happens to us. As students in the school of life, we are responsible *to* our crises. What can we learn from them? How can we grow through them?

It's important that we look at illness or other crises as an educator giving us the opportunity to enrich our spirits and expand our consciousness and not to judgmentally label them as something we've created out of an inevitable flaw within ourselves. Yes, we do things and feel feelings that deplete our immune systems and create a climate in which illness can flourish, and it's very important that we pay attention to taking care of our bodies and our beliefs. But, if we badger ourselves mercilessly about being responsible for crises, we often end up paralyzed by guilt and, consequently, learn nothing.

There is also the possibility that our crises are lessons we signed up for on a spiritual level, opportunities to advance our soul by choosing gentleness, empowerment, and serenity over judgment, victimization, or bitchiness. Who knows? None of us, really. What we do know is that we're all enrolled in Saint's School and we learn best when treated with gentle kindness.

I forgive myself for having crises.

Although I may not like them, I do learn from crises.

Anointing Ourselves with Tears

AS THE TURKISH PROVERB STATES, "SHE THAT conceals her grief finds no remedy for it." Grief concealed becomes grief congealed. Sorrow and pain shift and heal more readily when we anoint ourselves with the balm of tears.

It's a well-known scientific fact that tears shed in grief, anger, hopelessness, and contrition contain significant toxins, whereas tears shed in joy and awe do not. From these findings, it appears that tears have the capacity to cleanse the body. I believe they can cleanse the soul as well. On occasion we've all probably known that we needed a "good" cry. We feel the buildup of energy and intuitively know that release can be found in the goodness of tears. If we allow ourselves to weep, we often feel refreshed and revitalized.

Thirteenth-century German mystic Mechthild of Magdeburg wrote that "tears are a passing on of the river of grace." She believed that tears were God's divine energy flowing through us. Wouldn't it be wonderful if we could move into the heart of our feelings and let warm, moist tears cleanse our bodies and anoint our souls?

"Jesus wept" is the shortest verse in the Bible, set off to underscore its significance, I presume. Who was more in the river of grace than the enlightened

Christ? His example is a good one for us to follow.

When you have a few undisturbed minutes, gently put your hands over your heart and breathe in the words "I love you" and "I long for your healing." As you breathe deeply, give yourself permission to let tears flow freely if they want to come. It isn't necessary to know what your tears are about; it's simply important to release them.

There's a little story that suggests God saves each of our tears, turns them into pearls, and presents them to us when we enter heaven. Anointing ourselves with tears not only aids in healing, but allows us to add to our celestial string of pearls.

I gently allow myself to cry needed tears.

The Beloved cherishes my tears.

Touching the Hem

IT'S VERY IMPORTANT, AS WE MOVE THROUGH the morass of confusion and consternation often prevalent in Saint's School, that we have taproots from which to draw energy, support, and solace.

Although we need other people whom we can count on to support us, God, angels, and other ethereal beings are happy to provide these comforts when we open ourselves to them and ask for their help. In the Bible, followers of Christ believed that if they touched the hem of his robe, they would be healed, and they were right. Part of our task in becoming women of spirit is to create a goodly supply of *internal* hems to touch, hands to hold, and arms to enfold us as we move toward greater wholeness.

If you're not comfortable using Christ as the symbol for an all-compassionate Being in the following meditation, please replace him with a Being of your own choosing. Allow your eyes to drift gently closed and visualize the thoughts of your mind and the feelings of your heart as white goose down feathers flung free from a ruptured pillow. Allow the feathers to settle quietly on the calm surface of a beautiful lotus pond. If any ornery feathers insist on staying airborne, go after them with amusement and tenderly coax them to land on the unruffled water. Invite Christ to be with you by the pond. In ways that feel nurturing to you, rest, rejuvenate, and heal in his presence.

In a particularly difficult time in my life, I gained great solace from picturing myself sitting on the ground beside Jeshua (Jesus' Aramaic name, and one that is less loaded for me) and leaning my head on his knee as he stroked my hair, while I fingered the hem of his garment.

A visualization of this type can help create an ongoing relationship with a loving Being that can become a taproot of strength and comfort for us.

I rest in the presence of a loving being.

I am loved and comforted, and
I freely love and comfort others.

Lifting the Rocks

EVEN THOUGH WE CAN'T READILY SEE IT, LIFE teems under rocks. Turn over a rock and notice all the little critters scurrying about, doing the business of living.

So it is with us—life is teeming beneath the rocks of our day-to-day existence. Whether we are suffering from the weight of accumulated fatigue or have been ripped from the very ground of our being, it's encouraging to remember that these are fertile times for spiritual growth. New life abounds as we gather the strength and energy to lift painful rocks and examine the underbelly of our own psyches and spirits. Such exploration definitely isn't easy, but it is necessary for the evolution of our souls. We need the dark, fertile, moist soil of crisis to define ourselves. Without struggle, there is no energy to break the shell encasing the seeds of our new self, the soul-self that we are becoming.

Vulnerability is wrapped around the axis of all pain. Therefore, as we go into the darkness, it's crucial to do so gently. Kicking over inner rocks with a vengeance and squashing the little bug beings revealed only causes our spirits to wisely move out of reach.

With gentleness in mind, close your eyes and imagine yourself as light as a feather on the breath of God. Supported by the Divine, effortlessly float to a beautiful place in nature. When you see a spot where you would like to glide to a stop, softly settle into the beauty. Beside you is a rock that represents an experience or belief that causes you pain. Holding fast to the awareness of the sacred opportunity for soul growth in all experiences, turn over your rock and gently examine the insights to be exposed in the fertile darkness.

Carl Jung reminds us, "There is no coming to consciousness without pain." Would that that were not true, but it usually is. What radiant spiritual possibilities lie in the shadows of your rocky pain waiting to be unearthed?

I am gentle with myself as I turn over the rocks of my psyche.

*I open my heart to the opportunities
inherent in pain and crisis.*

Moving Toward Acceptance

I LOVE THE NORSE SAYING, "CLOUDS MOVE." It reminds me that no matter how many clouds cover the sun, they will eventually leave. It is their nature, just as it is the nature of the human spirit to move out from under clouds and heal in the wake of crisis and trauma. Continually and consciously moving toward acceptance of people and circumstances over which we have no control creates an atmosphere that supports healing and transformation. Although acceptance isn't easy, it is facilitated when we re-form and re-frame crisis through rewording how we think and talk about it.

A few simple, but helpful suggestions are:

1. Change "my" and "our" pain to "the" pain. The pain is less personal and more manageable.

2. Replace both the words and attitude of "Isn't it awful!" Instead, learn to say and believe, "That's good." We don't have to believe that something is good right away, and if we just can't bring ourselves to say "That's good," we can pray, "I can't yet see any good in this. Please help my vision clear and my trust return."

3. We can dis-identify with our feelings by remembering that at the core of ourselves is an indestructible divinity—our soul-self—who understands and remains apart from the crucible of crisis

(or, at least, remains unscathed and unscarred). We can help ourselves dis-identify with our pain and remember our Self by saying, "I have this feeling, but I am not this feeling. I am_____." I then fill that space with whatever feels the most healing. I use a "pure child of God" or "a strong and wise spiritual being." It varies with my need.

4. Remember, "This, too, shall pass." When this challenge has passed, what growth and insights will you have gleaned?

Clouds move, crises pass, wounds heal; acceptance helps.

Difficult feelings flow through me like clouds moving through the sky.

I am a survivor and thriver.

Sanctifying Pain

. . . .

> *Though the soul's wounds heal, the scars remain.*
> *God sees them not as blemishes but as honors.*
> —Julian of Norwich

MYSTICS AND PHILOSOPHERS AGREE THAT IT IS
pain that seasons and strengthens our souls. Pain
used as an impetus for soul growth and understanding is sanctified as a result. Staying open to the
honors to be gained from pain is difficult at the
onset of a wound. Our task, when first thrown to
the mat, is to gently allow ourselves to grieve and,
later when and if we're able, to be willing to open
to the soul growth inherent in the experience.

When initially faced with the knowledge that
my first marriage was on the rocks, I was devas-
tated and obsessed with the searing pain that I felt.
At first, if anyone had told me to open to the soul
growth in this experience, I would have wanted to
punch them out. Over time, and with much help, I
was able to accept that, from this crisis, a new and
better Sue might emerge. And that was the turning
point.

For me, Jung's statement, "It is through the
wounds that light can come in" was absolutely true.
In the fire of my pain was born the therapist I
became, the spiritual seeker that I still am, and the

person I quest to be. I can truthfully say that I feel extraordinarily blessed by the gifts that emanated from my divorce.

Paradoxically, there are still—and always will be—fragments of sadness to hold side by side with the gratitude. Sanctification of our pain requires that we embrace the paradox and give thanks for both the growth and sadness hidden in the mystery of Saint's School. Embracing all aspects of crisis makes it easier for our scars to become badges of honor.

Intermittently, life cracks us all open, and we heal stronger in the broken places. Today, what cracks and wounds would you like to invite the light to shine through by sanctifying the pain with growth and gratitude?

I accept joy and sorrow alike and learn from each.

I invite light to shine through my wounds, blessing others.

Soothing the Soul with Ritual

RITUAL IS IMPORTANT DURING CRISIS FOR IT is the language of the soul. In difficult times, ritual can help us reaffirm our relationship with the Divine, satiate our thirst for spiritual sustenance, and augment our flagging trust in the goodness of life.

I was very inspired by the rituals Julianna, a young woman whom I met at an Elisabeth Kubler-Ross workshop, shared with me. Afflicted with multiple sclerosis (MS), Julianna used Goodbye Rituals to formalize the letting go of the activities and functions of her body that she lost as her disease progressed. The first was a ceremony celebrating the years that she had been an avid rock climber and guided disadvantaged kids on adventures such as Outward Bound. To help her both grieve and celebrate her curtailed outdoor activities, she invited some of the people with whom she had gone on those excursions to her home. They shared memories, stories, anger, frustration, and tears.

The final segment of Julianna's ceremony included dividing her gear among the young people present and symbolically burning maps of her favorite trails and rock climbing spots. Julianna prayed that her feelings, fueled by the MS, be transformed and transmuted into acceptance and strength just as the maps were being transformed, by fire, into a different, more ethereal energy. Each time Julianna lost another activity or ability, she—with the help of her caretaker—ritualized the process of letting go and asked for God's help in living graciously until death. Not long before her death, she wrote me that creating and performing the rituals had been a major contributor to her eventual peace of mind and serenity. She graduated from Saint's School, Phi Beta Kappa, I bet.

Are there ways in which your soul could be soothed through ritual? If so, give yourself the blessing of creating one. It doesn't matter what we *do* in a ritual; our souls—the wise, inner source of our being—respond to our heartfelt intention.

I soothe my soul through ritual.
I am serene and have peace of mind.

Nurturing the Three F's

....

AS WE MOVE EVER HIGHER IN OUR COMMITMENT
to nurturing and enriching the spirit within us, we
learn to make daily choices for love and to priori-
tize our lives accordingly.

In reevaluating what has value and meaning to
them, almost all of the cancer and AIDS patients
that Dr. Joan Borysenko has worked with come up
with what she calls the Three F's: Faith, Family, and
Friends. I would include oneself in the "Friends"
category.

Each of these F's has to do with love—how we
connect with and relate to the Divine, ourselves,
and others. In my own hospice work, I've talked
with many terminally ill people who've told me
that although their illness was killing them, it was
also providing them with the incentive to live
from their hearts as their top priority. Faced with
imminent death, most of us don't decide to work
more—unless our work is a source of creativity and
meaning. What we usually realize, when setting
final priorities, is that we want to make profoundly
loving connections.

Long before death taps on our door, we can
choose to orient our lives according to the Three
F's. Today, take a sheet of paper and at the top,
jot down Family, Friends/Self, and Faith—or any

other heading that comes to you. Thoughtfully and tenderly list under each heading ways that you might choose to act differently if you, or any of the people in your life, were to be given only a year to live. I know this idea is commonplace, but actually performing the exercise can be extremely enlightening. Use it as a springboard for change, if needed, or as an affirmation, if appropriate.

Daily conscious decisions to choose love and to drink from the restorative well of Faith, Family, and Friends helps assuage our spiritual thirst for fulfillment and meaningful connections with ourselves, others, and our Source.

I fill myself at the well of love.
I tenderly nurture my faith, family, and friends.

Polishing Golden Souls

OUR SOULS ARE GOLDEN, AND OUR BACK-grounds either encourage them to shine or help them to tarnish. For those of us who feel we have spots of tarnish on our souls, there are many ways to polish them back to their natural radiance.

No matter how desperately we may hope for a better yesterday, the reality of the past cannot be changed. But the wonderful news is that the energy of the past *can* be transformed and transmuted, changed and lifted into the light of God. Through the incredible wisdom and creativity of our imagination, we can pluck painful or limiting fragments of energy from the barbed wire fences of our past and release them to express their perfect, right energetic vibration.

I learned the following soul-buffing technique from my spiritual mother, Annabelle Woodard. This meditation can be used to change the energy of any painful past experience, but I'm going to use it here in what Annabelle calls "Grafting a New Childhood." Please feel free to tailor the meditation to your own unique needs if you have no parental issues or if some other wound calls to you more clearly.

Make yourself comfortable and close your eyes. Focus your attention on your breath and allow it to deepen naturally. On the in-breath say, "I," and as you breathe out, say, "Invite healing." When you feel more relaxed and open, invite your mind to roam back into your childhood until you see or sense a scene that you would like to transform. Call in your guardian angels to protect and comfort you as you relive the scene as you remember it. And now ask the compassionate wisdom of your heart to help you craft a different scenario. The first step is to request that your ideal parents appear. With these new parents in place, redo the experience. You may change anything you want in order to create it exactly as you wish it had been, and, energetically speaking, you will make it so.

Transforming the energy of the past by recreating that which needs healing burnishes our souls to a golden hue.

My soul is a golden reflection of Spirit.

I deserve love, and I am capable of transforming painful energy into loving energy.

Changing Form, Not Essence

WHILE WATCHING THE SUN SET OVER THE Pacific Ocean on the anniversary of my dad's death, I had a comforting thought. Similar to foam on the breast of the ocean, we individuals are like foam in the sea of creation: mysteries, uniquely defined for a short space of time, and then absorbed back into the Source.

When we grasp the reality that no matter what form of foam we are, each of us is an integral part of the vast ocean and will become one with it in the natural ebb and flow of nature, fear loses its grip on us and our hearts open toward all of our brothers and sisters. Each form is equally ocean in essence—all important, precious, and sacred. There is no separation between us and God or between us and those we love who have changed from human form, even though visually and tactually there appears to be a separation.

There is a wonderful little chant that when sung repeatedly, helps us hold onto the belief of oneness with the Divine. As with most chants, this one is very simple: "I am a bubble, make me the sea. Make me the sea, oh make me the sea. I am a bubble, make me the sea."

I was singing this song and thinking about my dad when I was filled with the absolute assurance that Essence is forever, and we are all essence. Words are often inadequate to describe a heartfelt insight, and I feel that frustration now as the memory surges through me but the feelings refuse to be translated onto the page. My bet is that you understand anyway.

Our souls, like little kids, love repetition and bloom brilliantly when sacred words and thoughts are repeated. Let yourself get celestially creative and make up a tune to "I am a bubble, make me the sea," or compose your own unique refrain and sing it silently or aloud as you go through your day today. It's especially beneficial when negative thoughts are wreaking havoc in your heart. Your chant may become your heart-song.

I am one with the Divine.

*There is only the appearance of separation,
not separation itself.*

Walking Through *the Valley of the Shadow*

. . . .

WALKING THROUGH THE VALLEY OF THE shadow of death with someone can be a blessed experience, one that fills us with awe and gives us an undying belief in the eternal evolution of our souls. If sudden, however, the death of a loved one will, for a time, cast us into the fires of acute emotional trauma.

However, both peaceful and shocking deaths can bring forth an emergence of heart and soul. Our hearts, broken open by grief, bear fruits of the Spirit in the same way a seed, broken open by nature, bears fruits that sustains the body. As M.C. Richards says, "If you live into the experience of grief or loss deeply, you will perceive that what has taken place is not discontinuity but metamorphosis."

An essential quest for us is to discover beliefs about death that nourish us, for our attitudes surrounding the inevitability of the body's extinction either help or hinder our spiritual growth. The deeper our faith in the evolution of our souls and the benevolence of the Divine, the greater our acceptance of all circumstances and the possibility of transformation in them.

In all of my work with death and dying, one thing stands out as the most important in walking *through* the valley rather than being *stuck* in the shadows. And that is overcoming the fear of death. Those who do have faith in the eternality of the soul are transformed through the process of both grieving and dying themselves. Conversely, those who believe death is the end, struggle to regain their equilibrium when facing death or bereavement, and sometimes never do.

When I was younger, death was not something I thought about; indeed, it was something I avoided out of fear. As I've aged, I can truthfully say that I have come to feel as Pearl S. Buck does, "You are only afraid because you don't know anything about death. . . . But someday you will wonder why you were afraid, even as today you wonder why you feared to be born." Like the caterpillar, we are called upon to overcome our fear of death and emerge from the darkness transformed into more beautiful spiritual beings.

I accept death as merely another form of life.

My soul is eternal and indestructible.

Dancing with the Dead

IN SOME NATIVE AMERICAN TRADITIONS, IT IS believed that we dance with our ancestors along the Milky Way after we leave this life. So many of the stories I've heard and experiences I've had convince me that we don't have to leave this life in order to dance with those who have already departed. Although I've had several encounters with my mother's spirit since her death, I want to tell you about one particular "dance" that we shared.

Minutes after Mother's death, I was engulfed by a sense of euphoria that stayed with me constantly for ten days. Never before or since have I experienced such prolonged joy. At the time, I thought the feeling came from my relief at Mother's release from pain. Several years later, during a meditation, I casually asked why I had felt the way I had. Although I really didn't expect an answer, immediately an internal message came—clear as a bell: "It wasn't just relief, as you think, Honey. You brought me such comfort *during* the illness that I wanted to share with you a little of what I was feeling *after* it." If what I felt was death, it is truly a dance of ecstasy.

Befriending death allows our spirits much freer reign in life. Toward that end, please close your eyes and, in whatever way feels right to you, sink

GRATITUDE IS THE FINEST PRAYER OUR souls can utter. Gratitude is also an attitude. As with any attitude, it can be nurtured, cultivated, and changed if need be. Gratitude, like laughter and humor, lifts our spirits and hearts and encourages us to ascend into realms of joy and appreciation. It makes us thankful for the incredible gift of life that we've been given and for the people who have chosen to share it with us.

Gratitude gentles even the roughest roads and gives wings to the heart. Buoyed by gratitude, we can sail over most situations while keeping a healthy, and even joyful, perspective on the landscape of our lives. Gratitude is communion with God and graces our relationships with a high and holy soul-connection. Gratitude is meditation in action. Gratitude is the single most powerful medicine for physical, mental, and spiritual health for us individually and for our planet as a whole.

Drinking the Sweet Nectar
of Gratitude

. . . .

WE ARE OFFSPRING OF THE ALMIGHTY, FILLED
with divine energy and powerful potential. As we
gently learn to believe in our own worth, gratitude
for our unique individuality is the result.

Wine can give us a high and, regrettably, also a
headache. Drinking deeply of gratitude, on the
other hand, is naturally intoxicating, with no bad
aftereffects. This sweet nectar of the gods nurtures
our ability to ascend into the company of angels
and live life from our hearts, with freer access to
our soul-energy.

It might help to realize the value of gratitude
toward ourselves if we were to visualize our heart
as a delicate treasure, hand-blown from the rarest
ethereal glass. A treasure valuable beyond imagining—fragile, irreplaceable, priceless, and ancient.
There is *no* other like it—infinitely precious, exist-
ing before time and after infinity.

In reality, we *were* entrusted with such an inex-
plicable treasure when we were given the gift of
life. We, and our wonderful hearts, are infinitely
strong, vastly vulnerable, deserving and needing
the gentle touch of gratitude and love.

With your eyes closed, very gently put your

hands over your heart and allow your breath to tenderly flow in and out of it. When you feel ready, ask to be given a symbol for your heart. Hold the symbol that you see or sense as carefully and gently as you would a priceless Fabergé egg. Beholding the wonder of your symbol, allow gratitude to flow through you, permeating the very cells of your being. Make a commitment with yourself to cherish and appreciate your heart-self.

We also need to be especially gentle with ourselves when we misplace our sense of gratitude. We are human, and, when the pain in our hearts becomes acute, we sometimes forget to be grateful. That's okay, because we can always reclaim our gratitude. And as we remember to drink the sweet nectar of gratitude toward ourselves, the cup naturally passes to those whom we love.

I am infinitely grateful for my heart and soul.
Daily, I drink the sweet nectar of gratitude.

Nibbling Back to God's Pastures

DISTRACTED AND OVERBUSY, WE CAN EASILY become like sheep and, with our heads down, inadvertently nibble our way out of God's pastures. Often, when we take the time to look up, we're astounded at how far afield we've wandered. Fortunately, gratitude is a surefire way to nibble our way back when we meander away from our spiritual home.

In the wake of losing her job, Ruth, a single woman in her thirties, battled insomnia during the night and exhaustion spiked with panic during the day. Finally, in desperation, she got up one late evening and numbly made a list of all the things that she had to be thankful for. Although she didn't *feel* thankful, she prayed for the strength to overcome her fear and the grace to experience gratitude. No bolts of lightning struck that night, but when she returned to bed, she did fall asleep. Getting up and at least thinking about being thankful became a ritual for Ruth when sleep eluded her. Slowly—nibble by minuscule nibble—she began to really feel gratitude and, with it, the ballast of hope.

It's said that "Thank you" is the most powerful prayer, and thank yous are invariably connected with gratitude. The following exercise can help illuminate the path back to the pastures for which we yearn.

Very quickly jot down all of the things for which you are thankful. The list may include people, ideas, objects—whatever pops into your mind. Once you have your list, say a tiny thank you for each item on the paper.

To be really creative, make a Thank You Box and toss in ideas or experiences for which you are thankful every day. In the finest sense of the word, this is a Prayer Box; each slip of paper placed in it and every little "thank you" murmured over it are nibbles back toward God's pastures.

God waits for us by the gates of gratitude.

I am grateful for all that I am and all that I have been.

I am at home in God.

Cultivating Optimism

AN OPTIMISTIC ATTITUDE INVITES AN INFLUX OF positive energy into ourselves. You might say that optimism is the yeast in the bread of life. With it we rise, without it our spirits fall flat.

By her own admission, Cecilia is a recovering pessimist. She came by it naturally through the litanies she often heard repeated by her family of origin: "Isn't that terrible? Wouldn't you know it" (usually accompanied by a sigh); "Well, what can you expect from a politician, teenager, mail- man . . ." (or whatever hapless person was skew- ered at the moment); "It doesn't get much worse than this," and, finally, "Lord knows I tried!" (always accompanied by a sigh).

After living in another state for several years, Cecilia was having lunch in her hometown with her aunt, cousin, and mother. Because she had been away, she was struck by the pessimistic and nega- tive tenor of the talk around the table as never before. "I sat there stunned," she told me, "nause- ated, heavyhearted, and longing to escape. Starting right then, I vowed to become an optimist." It must have worked because Cecilia is fun to be around, and two of the adjectives often used to describe her are "optimistic" and "lighthearted."

Darkness and heaviness weigh us down and clog

our hearts and arteries physically, emotionally, and spiritually. An Irish proverb states, "A light heart lives long," but afflicted by a dark attitude and a heavy heart, life, no matter how long it really is, *seems* endless, dreary, and bleak.

Luckily, neither heavyheartedness nor a pessimistic attitude needs to be a life sentence. We can learn to "enlighten up" as an astute bumper sticker teaches. We can transform a bad habit into a good one by consistently and gently monitoring our self-talk and changing any negative pessimism we spot to positive optimism. We can revive our spirits by cultivating optimism.

I am lighthearted and optimistic.

Life is great.

Distilling Wine from Sour Grapes

IN AESOP'S FABLE, THE FOX, AFTER FUTILE EFFORTS to reach a juicy clump of grapes, scorns them as being sour. I can imagine him haughtily turning up his nose and swishing his tail as he harrumphs away, belittling the coveted fruit only because he can't have it.

How often do we, like Mr. Fox, sully our spirits by falling prey to the sour-grape syndrome of jealousy, envy, or judgment of ourselves as not being up to snuff? I for one was plagued by jealousy as a youngster, and it made my life—and me, I suspect—miserable. Luckily, sour grapes are no longer a daily snack.

Another success story that I'd like to share with you concerns fraternal twins Penny and Pam. The girls couldn't have been more disparate if they'd been born in different families. For most of their childhood, Pam was terribly jealous of Penny and, because of her feelings of inferiority, belittled her sister both in private and in public, generally trying to make her life miserable. At her wit's end, Penny came to see me when she was a junior in high school. In therapy, she learned how to protect herself from her sister's barbs while also accepting responsibility for her part of the sour-grape syndrome.

Eventually, Pam joined her sister in therapy. A great deal of their work concentrated on increasing their individual self-esteem, being thankful for their differences, and viewing dissimilarities as ways to complement each other rather than compete. As adults, Pam and Penny continue to be completely different from each other, but they also enjoy a full-bodied and robust friendship.

If you find a sour grape fermenting in your mouth, it's wise to immediately change its es-sence with a little prayer or thought of gratitude. Wine distilled from sour grapes is often sweeter because of the spiritual discipline of thankfulness required to make the transformation.

I am happy being exactly who I am.
I am thankful for all that comes my way
and look for the good in it.

Kissing the Joy

To pour the sacred water of the Beloved upon our spirits we must first, *recognize* joy as it brushes lightly against our souls, and second, *appreciate* joy in the moment without trying to snatch it and bury it in the backyard like a bone. William Blake describes this beautifully in his poem, "Kiss the Joy as It Flies."

> *He who binds to himself a joy*
> *Does the winged life destroy,*
> *But he who kisses the joy as it flies*
> *Lives in eternity's sunrise.*

If we feel less joy in our lives than we do guilt, obligation, resentment, exhaustion, or depression, it probably means that a spiritual tune-up is in order. We may simply need to recalibrate our ability to tune into joy as it flits unobtrusively by the windows of our souls.

Daily, joy sits patiently on the sill, gently fanning its wings waiting for us to recognize it. But oblivious or blinded by our own agenda, we sometimes act as C. S. Lewis lamented to a friend, "It seems to me that we often, almost sulkily, reject the good that God offers us because, at that moment, we expected some other good."

After tuning our intention toward recognizing the good that God offers, it's important that we hold its fragile essence in an open hand, accepting and appreciating it now, not crushing it in a clenched fist in hopes of preserving it for later.

That true joy is sufficient unto the moment is hard to remember. I know, because Blake's poem settled itself in my broken heart during a black period when joy was hard to come by. Nonetheless, his poem became a spiritual challenge to me. For its inspiration, I am eternally grateful. Appreciating and then releasing joy allows us, paradoxically, to truly savor it.

I open my eyes to joy.

Each day I become more gifted at recognizing joy.

Tethering Our Hearts to God

RELATIONSHIPS ARE THE THREADS WITH WHICH God weaves our earthly world. The ways we relate to and care for each other create the pattern from which our society is fashioned. When relationship strands are weak, the very fabric of life becomes frayed. Therefore, if we're to have the cohesive, creative, and peaceful existence for which we yearn, we need to strengthen and deepen our close relationship ties with God, ourselves, and others.

Our ability to love others unconditionally grows out of our ability to open our hearts to both ourselves and to God. When we tether our hearts to the heart of the Beloved, our relationships become threads worthy of the loom of God.

The following meditation has been helpful for my clients and myself when we seem to be disconnected from God and are floating untethered in a vast and shadowy void.

Gently close your eyes and place your hands over your heart. Concentrate on breathing deeply and evenly while allowing tension to melt and flow away from your body. If your mind wanders, simply return your focus to your breath. Aloud, either say or sing, "Mother/Father God (or use a name with which you resonate), please show me anything that separates me from thee." Utter this prayer from deep within the core of your heart, truly yearning for the answer. Open yourself to insights, awarenesses, or symbols; then ask your wise heart and guardian angels to help you heal and bless whatever appears to be separating you from God.

In the perfect, right way for you, visualize an exquisite cord emanating from your heart into the heart of the Beloved. Feel the energy of unconditional love flowing between you. From your sanctified and overflowing heart, send out a rush of gratitude to those you love, to God, and to all of Her creations.

I am eternally and joyfully connected to God.

My life is woven from threads of love.

Sending Appreciation

. . . .

WE'VE ALL HEARD ABOUT POURING OIL ON troubled waters, and, when we generously pour the oil of appreciation onto our lives and loves, there will be fewer troubled waters for us to wade through. The oil of appreciation energizes all it touches, for appreciation comes from the heart, which is the throne of the Spirit.

One of the best ways to build our appreciation muscles is to bless everything and everyone, especially our family and friends. Without the oil of appreciation, our relationships with family and friends can become dry and chafing.

When Sonya first came to see me, she was puzzled about why it was difficult for her to be around her father. He was a nice, respectable man and a good father, but she felt inadequate and uncomfortable in his presence. Eventually it dawned on Sonya that her dad never said anything complimentary to her. Although he was polite and mouthed "thank yous," he never highlighted any personal positives of Sonya's. In therapy, Sonya realized how much she longed to be told by her dad what, if anything, he appreciated about her and her accomplishments. Although she could not change who he was, she did learn from the experience to shower others with her appreciation.

To practice sending appreciation, center your awareness in your heart and rest there for a few minutes with no expectations, just breathe in and out. In your mind's eye allow yourself to go to a beautiful place. Glancing around, appreciate the beauty and charm of the place you have chosen. After a minute, very gently begin to appreciate yourself, both for who you are and for your willingness to learn and grow. Invite family members and friends to join you in this meditation. Send appreciation to each one. For a difficult person, find at least one characteristic or one tiny action that you can appreciate. If the waters between you are very troubled, you may only be able to appreciate how many times they have given you the opportunity to practice patience.

By sending silent strands of appreciation we bless others and strengthen the bonds between us and them and between ourselves and our spirits.

I find something to appreciate about everyone.
I deserve to be blessed by appreciation from others.

Being Thankful for Aging

IF OLD AGE IS THE VERDICT OF LIFE, GRATITUDE softens the verdict. Overturning the youth-is-panacea verdict pronounced by our society is a crucial spiritual requirement of our time, one that will enable us to reap the fruits of wisdom from each season.

The feminine Spirit deeply understands the natural cycles of life and welcomes them with reverence. In reuniting with our own innate spiritual wisdom we, too, will gracefully journey through the seasons until we grow into the simple elegance of winter and soar to the benevolent mystery of death.

It's early autumn as I write this; ripe fruits and vegetables beckon from roadside stands and trees shyly announce their intention to sleep. I love this time of year. Perhaps it's because I am an early autumn age, but there's something else—a promise of glory—awesome, breathtaking foliage made even more poignant by its being a prelude to the stark, bare branches of winter that have an elegant and uncomplicated beauty of their own. It is a cycle we trust. Spring will follow winter.

Author May Sarton expressed the beauty of aging when she said in her later years: "Old age is not an illness, it is a timeless ascent. As power diminishes, we grow more toward the light." And, isn't *that* power—to grow toward and be closer to the all-loving Light?

Sit quietly for a moment, breathe deeply, and draw into your body and soul a sense of peaceful gratitude. Allow your mind to float back over the ages you have grown through and, with gratitude, bless them for the joy experienced, the sorrow weathered, and the wisdom gathered. Now invite a picture or sense of who you will be at older ages to come into your mind's eye. Bless this woman as she bridges age to age. Encourage her to flower into the unique and beautiful bloom she is meant to be. Tap into her native strength as she begins to wilt physically. Treasure her essence, which is an eternal fragrance.

*I am thankful for each day that I am blessed
to live upon Mother Earth.*

I reap the harvest of wisdom from each season of my life.

Subsidizing Our Spirit by Paying Bills with Thanks

. . . .

ONE OF THE BEST WAYS TO DRINK FROM THE wellspring of Spirit is to adopt the attitude: *All that I do is spiritual.* Being waylaid by spiritually depleting beliefs in lack and meaninglessness is enervating and leads to feelings of discouragement. On the other hand, realizing that everything we do can be seen as spiritual and acting as such bolsters our spirits with enthusiasm and a sense of purpose.

We can go to the wellspring of Spirit with a Dixie cup punched full of holes by worry, resentment, or a half-empty mentality, or we can lift a chalice to the Source that is lined with a watertight belief in the sacredness of all things.

For Janice, a successful real estate broker, her hole-punching nemesis was writing the monthly alimony check to her former husband. As the first of the month approached, her jaws began to tighten and by the time she wrote the actual check she was a resentment-ridden mess. After a concerned friend asked her, "Who is this hurting?" Janice began to wonder how she could bypass the pain of paying that loathsome bill. For the first two months, she had the money automatically deducted from her account, but she still obsessed about it, "He probably got the money today, the jerk!" Who was still being hurt? Punch, punch, drip, drip, leak, leak.

Knowing that gratitude could lift her spirits, Janice finally decided to pretend to write "Thank you" on the memo line of the alimony check. "Thank you for being out of my life"; "Thank you for my lessons in what kind of man *not* to choose" were two of her first unwritten acknowledgements. But a funny thing happened. Eventually, she really did feel thankful, and sending off the check became a ritual of appreciation for all that she had learned from the relationship. She was free.

Through each everyday experience we can draw from the infinite well of Spirit. What size cup will you take to the well today?

All that I do is sacred.

I pay bills with a "Thank you."

Dining with Detractors

PEOPLE WHO ARE THE BIGGEST DETRACTORS IN our lives are often also our most valuable teachers. Out of the wounds inflicted by these severe critics, harsh teachers, and wielders of heavy and harmful blows can come much of our compassion and the majority of our strength. Without question, given a preview of coming detractions, we probably would-n't have invited such folks, or the resultant pain, into our lives. Nonetheless, we are indebted to them for the heart-growing, soul-tempering wisdom derived from our relationship with them.

Gracing these severe teachers with the blessing of gratitude frees us, and them, to move on to softer and sweeter experiences. A wonderful way to say good-bye and sever the connection spiritu-ally is to invite our detractors to dinner, in medita-tion. Before the event takes place, make careful preparations. First and foremost, decide how you will protect yourself while sharing psychic space with these people. Then compile your guest list; who will be seated where and by whom? What will be served? How will the table look?

When the preparations are finished, invite them to enter and take their seats. Observe these persons who have caused you pain, and carefully make an inventory of the gifts that they (no doubt, inadvertently) have given you in terms of soul growth and personality polishing. Thank each one of them for their contribution to your evolution. If you can't actually feel gratitude, ask the Beloved to open your heart so that gratitude toward them can seep into your soul.

Believe me, I am personally aware that this is not an easy dinner to hostess. Although I do feel thankful for lessons learned from her, I've not yet been able to invite one of my family members to share my psychic table. But I intend to do so one day for she taught me much, and I don't want to drag her energy with me throughout eternity.

Thankfulness helps heal our scars from the inside out and unveil the gifts of wisdom and compassion gleaned from receiving them.

I give thanks for my teachers.

I am stronger in the places where I've been wounded.

Embracing Angels
and Other Emissaries

*For he shall give his angels charge over you,
to keep you in all your ways.
They shall bear you up in their hands, lest
you dash your foot against a stone.*

—*Psalms 91:11–12*

OUR SPIRIT WANTS TO SURRENDER TO that which it perceives as higher and holier than itself. We need noble role models, and God is hard to visualize. To resolve this dilemma, and yet not singe our circuits to a frazzle with Her overwhelming power and majesty, I think the Beloved encourages angels and other emissaries to intercede on Her behalf. A widely held belief affirms that at least two angels are entrusted with our care at birth, and that others, including the Archangels themselves, are happy to assist us when we call upon them.

I have never seen an angelic being with my physical eyes, but I know several very down-to-earth people who have. On several occasions, however, I have been lovingly protected and guided by invisible, but obviously present, forces. I like to think that these forces were angels, celestial beings of some kind, or energy from my own higher Self. Given my experiences, and others I've heard about, I can't help but believe that just outside of our range of perception we are encircled by angels or guides, the spirits of those whom we have loved and lost, and emissaries from our personal soul-selves. And with that certainty comes incredible peace of mind.

Waiting in the Wings

YES, ALL THE WORLD'S A STAGE AND ALL THE men and women merely players, as Shakespeare said, but we are also the writers, producers, and directors of our life's play. Luckily, angels wait in the wings to be our prompters, guides, companions, and healers.

Running late, Maggie sprinted through the halls of the hospital, thinking only about where she would get gas for her car's empty tank after she finished visiting this patient. Imagine her amazement when she dashed through the door of the woman's room and saw an angel bending over the sleeping figure. The angel looked up, also surprised, smiled, and vanished. A child of the sixties, Maggie said, "Whoa! I've never experienced such a rush out of *anything* like I did out of seeing that angel!"

Not as dramatic, but nonetheless welcome, was an encounter I had one inky night alone in my car. Coming home from a pottery class, I decided to take an out-in-the-boonies shortcut that I'd only used previously during the day. Presumably, to forestall such shortcuts, someone had barricaded the little road and I was forced to turn around. When I backed up, my car fell in a hole and I was "turtled" helplessly on a hump, wheels in a hole and undercarriage caught on who knew what. It was pitch black and I was quite a long way from home.

Panicking, I called out to my mother who had been dead for several years. "Mother, it's Sue and my car and I are in trouble! Please help me! . . ." Daring to hope, I gunned the motor again, the car popped out of the hole and I made it home safely. Gene and I went back to check the hole the next day. My tire tracks were there and he said, "Only a miracle got you out of that hole." Yes, one performed by an angel waiting in the wings.

Today, cheer and comfort yourself by knowing that, just behind the curtain, your angels wait to help enhance your life's play.

I have angels waiting in the wings.

It's perfectly okay to ask for help.

Opening the Windows

. . . .

"GOD, WHOSE LOVE AND JOY ARE PRESENT everywhere, can't come to visit you unless you art there!" I love that wise adage from Meister Eckhart; it so succinctly states the obvious. By throwing open the windows of our souls through awareness and quiet contemplation, we will be able to welcome God's calling cards of light, love, joy, and solace.

Although daylight will peep through a very small hole, how much better to fling the windows of our souls wide in welcome to angels and other emissaries who come bearing gifts. The Beloved has a keen sense of humor and drama, and celestial callers can appear quite unexpectedly. We have to be on the lookout.

Diane felt restless and lonely one sunny day several months after the death of her mother and decided to take a drive. Admittedly feeling sorry for herself, she was lamenting how much she wished she could see her mother and know that she was all right. Suddenly, swooping in front of the car, sun gleaming on its white head, came an eagle (often said by native peoples to be messengers from the Great Spirit). Diane stopped the car and watched the eagle settle in the top of a tree. As she whispered, "Mom, is that you?" the eagle swiveled its head disdainfully and looked down as if to say, "Of course not! But she did send me." Diane laughed and felt her heart lift.

Tom, a conservative older gentleman, hesitantly revealed to me that his wife had appeared to him as her casket was being lowered into the ground. "I must have imagined it!" he said, "But the funny thing is, when she smiled at me, I got the feeling that I just might be able to make it through this."

Believed in or doubted, anticipated or unexpected, angels and other emissaries will fly through the open windows of our souls, lifting our hearts in the process.

Angels love me and look out for me.

I open the windows of my soul to welcome light and love.

Finding Peace in Silence
and Solitude

. . . .

THE OVERSTIMULATION OF TOO MUCH BUSY-
ness chafes our souls and makes it impossible for us
to recognize any angels gracing our lives. If we're
constantly rubbing shoulders with others, rarely
alone, seldom awash in silence but often engulfed
by outside demands, we can become irritated and
afflicted with what I call diaper rash of the soul.
Red, raw, and ugly low-grade pain, usually hidden
from view.

Itchy and irritated feelings are clues that we
need to close the door on chaos and take time to
rest, replenish, and restore our own souls. For most
of us, it's in the quiet company of our selves that we
are most likely to be soothed by the peaceful caress
of caring angels. Metaphorically fanned by the soft
wings of silence and solitude, we can cool our
frenzy, quiet our minds, and mellow our attitudes.
In silence, it's possible to drink deeply from the
pure well of peace waiting at the center of our souls.

White Eagle, a wonderful Native American
teacher, has this to say about finding peace, "You
long for peace. You think of peace as being good-
will among the nations, the laying down of arms.
But peace is far more than this, it can only be

understood and realized within your heart. It lies beneath all the turmoil and noise and clamor of the world, beneath feeling, beneath thought. It is found in the deep, deep silence and stillness of the soul. It is spirit; it is God."

Find a place and time when you can arrange for silence and solitude. For some of us, the best we can do is a few extra minutes locked in the bathroom. That's okay. Close your eyes and softly sigh into the silence. If there is background noise, listen to the silence between sounds. Concentrate on your heart, and follow a welcoming pathway deep into it. The path ends at a beautiful well. Rest there. Replenish. In peace-filled solitude, drink in the stillness of your soul.

Peace is the Goddess softly whispering to our souls.

I give myself permission to close the door on chaos.

I rest and replenish with silence and solitude.

Expecting Holiness from God Alone

. . . .

> *It is not because angels are holier than men or devils*
> *that makes them angels, but because they do not*
> *expect holiness from another, but from God alone.*
> —William Blake

ISN'T THE ABOVE STATEMENT A PERFECT ONE FOR those of us who tend to be perfectionists? According to Blake, we can don angelic robes simply by giving up our expectations of perfect holiness from ourselves! Merely surrendering into the reality that we are flawed, imperfect, and yet marvelously miraculous humans will actually advance us a rung or two up Jacob's ladder.

Being a recovering perfectionist, I find Blake's idea very appealing. Each time I'm more gentle with myself and others, can I tuck a little white feather into my symbolic wings? If I give up perfection as a prerequisite for worthiness and being lovable, will it put some spit and polish on my halo? Can learning to laugh good-humoredly at my foibles help me fly a little higher? Probably so.

Let's try it right now and see. Allow your eyes to close gently and your breath to deepen. As you inhale, draw in a sense of acceptance for yourself exactly as you are now. As you exhale, release any judgments and criticisms of yourself and ask your angels to transform the energy of perfectionism into the ideal energy for your soul's evolution. Without being critical of yourself, think of a time when your quest for perfection made you or someone else unhappy or uncomfortable. As if you had already given up expecting perfection and holiness from yourself, replay the encounter in precisely the way you would have liked it to be. Imagine yourself in a celestial costume shop and, for every step away from perfectionism you took in the replay, clothe yourself in a piece of angel raiment.

God's job description includes holy perfection; ours does not.

I accept and love myself as I am.
I accept and love others as they are.

Reflecting the Face of God

. . . .

AS WOMEN OF SPIRIT, WE ARE GIVEN THE opportunity to reflect the face of God to those whom we love and to those whose lives we breeze through briefly. What does the face of God reflect? Of course, we're not altogether certain, but let's assume that God is love far beyond our ability to envision. In that case, Her face would surely reflect unconditional love, a wish to bless all of her children, a longing to bring solace to those seared by pain, an acceptance of the bumblings and stumblings natural to emotional and spiritual growth, and a desire to encourage and support creative efforts.

Most of us are already gifted at reflecting the face of God. And we can become even dearer blessings by more closely following the urgings of our hearts which are, in essence, reflections of the Divine.

All morning, the image of a woman whom Molly only slightly knew kept popping into her mind. Because she had been touched by reading portions of the woman's latest book, she dismissed the urge to call, thinking that her mind was just ruminating on the ideas in the book. Unable to shake the urge to call the author, Molly asked her heart for guidance. "Call!" came the immediate message. When Molly phoned and thanked the writer for the beauty of the book and for the hope that it had instilled in her, the woman burst into tears. It turned out that the author was having one of those down-in-the-dumps, doubting days when she wondered if her work was worth the effort and if anyone really benefited from it. She sorely needed encouragement. By listening to the wise angel-urgings of her heart, Molly became a blessing to the author and, in doing so, reflected the face of God.

Acting from our hearts brushes us all with the gentle wings of love. What loving act can you make today?

I listen and act on the urgings of my heart.

To the best of my ability, I reflect the face of God to others.

Asking for Guidance

. . . .

AROUND US, AND WITHIN OUR HEARTS AND
souls, resides a plethora of helpers willing to pour
forth a wealth of insight. At any time we can ask
for inspiration, instruction, and understanding, and
angels and other emissaries will respond. Granted,
their answers are often subtle and devilishly hard
to decipher. To help us trust in the authenticity of
angelic help and the reality of receiving inspiration
and instruction, prayers and meditations like the
following are invaluable.

Tamilou, a spiritually dedicated young woman,
uses this beautiful prayer when feeling the need for
special guidance. To prepare, Tamilou randomly
selects an Angel Card and casts a circle of light
around herself. Then she prays, "Dear Goddess,
please give me divine knowledge, divine wisdom,
and divine guidance. Give me the truth, not my
wishful thinking or my worst fears." Having asked
for what she wants, Tamilou becomes receptive by
silently meditating or writing in her journal. While
the answers she seeks are only rarely immediate or
obvious, they do appear eventually.

A meditation that I find both helpful and soul-
lifting is to envision meeting a person, or persons,
with whom I resonate spiritually. For me, such a
beloved wisdom teacher might be Christ (or Jeshua,

as his family called him), a Being named The Lady, or the Mother Mary as the strong, wise, and gentle woman I have come to believe that she was and is.

If you can, turn within now. Magnetize your energy back to your own body, heart, and spirit from all of the places it has been dispersed today. Think of a spiritual being with whom you resonate. Meet them in a beautiful place that is comfortable for you both and be with them in the ways that feel right for you now. You may want guidance or you may need solace and comfort. Ask for what you want and need.

Angels and other emissaries want to serve us. Our challenge is to believe and ask.

Beloved and blessed wisdom teachers please guide me.

I believe my prayers are answered.

Invoking Archangels

I WANT TO SHARE A WONDERFUL PRAYER invoking the four archangels, which is adapted from an ancient, mystical Jewish prayer. In it, we call in the archangels Uriel, Michael, Raphael, and Gabriel to encircle us with their presence. Please feel free to personalize it to suit yourself.

First, I invoke the angel Uriel in front of me, focus on that area and try to feel his loving presence. Uriel is the angel of clarity and discrimination, and I pray something like this, "Uriel, please clear my mind. Help me have clarity of vision, purity of heart, and wise discrimination." If I'm confused about a particular issue, I'll ask for clarity with it.

Then, on my right side, I call for Michael, who is the angel of love and loving kindness. I always like to bask in his presence for a few minutes before asking, "Michael, please show me how to open my heart in true loving kindness, especially when I feel fundamentally unloving. Help me graciously accept your love and the love of others, and guide me in the right way to love myself, others, and the world. Flow through me, please."

On my left side, I invoke the angel Gabriel, who brings strength and helps overcome fear. If I have a special fear or need, I pray about it. If not, I just ask for strength in general.

Behind me is Raphael, the angel of healing. I ask him to care for any of my specific ills or concerns, and then I invite him to care for the healing needs of others. I also invite him to move into my body, permeating all of my being with his healing energy.

After invoking the four archangels, I ask that their love flow into my heart and then out to others who are in need of help and blessing. During the day, I try to remember their nearness and feel their closeness.

Archangels Uriel, Michael, Gabriel, and Raphael
love to answer when I call.

I am encircled by angelic love.

Blessings from Cherubs

POLLY ARRIVED AT HER SON'S PRESCHOOL A little early, so she sat down with him and his friends at the snack table. Three-year-old Jeremiah, who is so adorable that he could be an artist's model posing for cherubs, put his arm around his mother, looked up at her, and said, "I was in heaven with God and he gave me a choice of moms, and I chose you!"

Any mother would be thrilled with such a statement, but it was a heart-lifting blessing for Polly because at that moment she was in the throes of struggling with chronic depression and low self-esteem and felt as if she could hardly drag herself through the day. Her son's comment brightened the gathering darkness. In his own angelic way, Jeremiah had assured his mom that she was a beautiful being, worthy of love. Indeed, *chosen* for love.

Whenever you get the chance, gather a blessing from a cherub. If you do not have children of your own, chortle at a baby in the grocery store and let her smile light up your day. Wave to children as they play. Find a painting or card of a darling baby and put it where his innocence can twinkle at you.

If there are no little ones, fresh from God, in your life, you can invite their presence through creative imagination. Softly close your eyes and allow your breath to deepen. Let your imagination soar into a realm where the Beloved Mother is playing with a number of babies. Be content to merely observe the scene until you feel especially drawn to one or two of the cherubs and then, in a way that feels comfortable to you, join them. Absorb the blessing of their joyous purity, and be cheered by their delight in you.

As a new grandmother, I've come to believe that being anointed by the blessing of cherubs is experiencing a love similar to the pure, unconditional love with which the Beloved holds us.

There is within me a pure and joyous cherub.

The Beloved loves me unconditionally.

Catching God's Drift

. . . .

SPIRIT IS ALWAYS COMMUNICATING WITH US VIA intuition, but regularly we don't catch the drift. Maybe we're deafened by the roar of demands from family and work or too busy elsewhere to interpret symbols when they appear, feel the soft breeze of God's loving caress, or hear the silent insights whispered in our ears by angels. As Antoine de Saint-Exupery explained in *The Little Prince*, "It is only with the heart that one can see rightly; what is essential is invisible to the eye." Therefore, it is by making space for ourselves and opening our hearts in awareness that we more easily catch God's drift.

Animals are favorite emissaries of spiritual messages. One morning I was walking by a stream, concentrating on opening my heart by singing the chant, "Lord, please let me see anything that stands between me and thee." I rounded a corner and saw two wolves looking down at me from a wildlife-rescue facility across the water. The largest wolf was white and the smaller, black. Touched, my knees started shaking.

Seeing the wolves was especially moving to me because I have had recurring dreams in which a white and a black wolf play the central parts. To me they are guardians of my well-being, symbols of masculine and feminine divine energy. Staring at these magnificent beings, I felt seen and cared for by the Spirit within me and the unfathomable mystery surrounding me. The message I caught was, "I hear you. I am as close as breath and as far as your disregard and distraction."

Today, please give yourself the essential gifts of an open heart and quiet time alone in nature—a small corner of a garden or loving and appreciating a houseplant; even looking at the moon and stars through the window is fine if you are housebound or live in the city. We catch the drift of heavenly communion in the sacred center of our open hearts.

Lord, please help me see anything that comes between me and thee.

God is as close as my breath.

Creating and Accepting Sanctuary

The very seams of my soul
Feel frayed by the weight of
                    death
                          business
                                  loneliness

I long to collapse in
              angels' arms
And let them gently knit me
Back together

I WROTE THE ABOVE POEM WHILE LONGING for a sanctuary of solace and support. We all go through times when we need a metaphorical—and sometimes actual—lap to crawl into and lay down our weary heads. For emotional and spiritual health, we require friends whom we can count on to provide strength when we are vulnerable, comfort when we are aching, and guidance when we are confused. We all need spiritual sisters whose wings are powerful enough for two when ours are limp and useless. More than likely you provide a lap and wings for others, but do you have angel's arms in which to collapse if need be?

If the answer is yes, wonderful. If it is no, it is possible *and* essential to create such support.

Desiree was worn out by countless family demands and badly needed a friend to bounce her feelings off of. It was late and she didn't want to disturb me by calling, so in her imagination she invited me to sit across from her for tea and conversation. "I" just listened at first, Desiree said, and then gave her some good suggestions about how to take care of herself. Although she knew that I wasn't there in person, she felt much better after our "conversation."

What a great lesson for all of us! If friends are physically unavailable, we can conjure up an *internal* soul-sister or angel and allow her to be our sanctuary. The important thing is that we encourage ourselves to create sanctuaries in which to heal, rest, and replenish. The soul of spiritual friendship, like the sole of a shoe, allows us to walk on rocks with less pain.

I love myself enough to ask for support.
I provide a lap and wings for myself and others.

Entering the Harbor of Hope

. . . .

HOPE IS AN ANGELIC ATTITUDE. IT HELPS US SEE silver linings hidden within dark clouds and rise above trial, tribulation, and disappointment. Without hope, our spiritual light is doomed to be very dim, as Dante suggested in the *Inferno* when he wrote that the sign over the entrance to Hell read, "Abandon hope all ye who enter here."

Hope is a safe harbor in which we can find refuge when the storms of life roughly toss us around or the flotsam and jetsam of frustration batters our hulls. I have had times in my life when I felt so engulfed by misery that I didn't know if I could keep my nose above water one more day. At one point, if it hadn't been for my children, I may not have had the courage to stay in the fray. Like sand in an hourglass, hope had drained from my spirit. Luckily, I had life-jackets other than my children, and they held me up until I could tread a little water under my own power. As I regained strength, the following meditation helped reinforce my spiritual ballast.

Gently close your eyes and focus on your breath, allowing it to float effortlessly in and out. With each inhalation, imagine that you are drawing the energy of hope into your body and soul. It doesn't matter if you feel hopeful, the intention toward hopefulness is enough for now. Briefly, think of any circumstance, feeling, or belief that is creating stormy seas for you. Notice that a short distance away is a quiet, serene, and welcoming harbor. Angels, friends, or other emissaries beckon for you to come into the harbor and, intuitively, you know that increased serenity and calm waits for you there. As you enter the harbor of hope, you are greeted by Beings who will care for you compassionately. Rest with them and allow them to minister to you.

When you are anointed with the angelic attitude of hope, raging seas are calmed and balance and harmony is restored.

I am a woman filled with hope.

I turn to friends and angels for infusions of hope.

Becoming the Arms of God

WE ARE GOD AND GODDESS' ARMS PRESENT IN the world. Who needs a hug? Who needs a heart-lift? Whose groceries need to be bought? Who needs a willing ear to listen to their story? Whose rights need to be championed? Who needs a hand to hold? When we offer our arms (or hearts and ears) for these services, we are offering a tangible fragment of God's love to one of her children. We will, as the hymn says, be like "angels descending, bring from above, echoes of mercy, whispers of love."

Each morning, before getting out of bed, Brenda breathes a request to the Divine. "Beloved Friend, I open myself to be of service. Please help me be your arms and willingly hold those who need a healing touch. Open my eyes that I may see what you ask of me today. Open my ears that I may truly hear and respond to the cries of joy and sorrow from your children. May the words of my mouth be the meditations of your heart, and may I sow peace wherever I go. Thank you."

Expressing and acting out our soul's angelic energy—becoming a circle of love for ourselves and others—is one of our highest callings. In living a life of spirit, we are challenged to surrender to the highest and holiest within us and become an advocate, a guardian angel of protection and strength, and a comforter for our dear friend, self, and for those whose lives we touch. Although we may question our ability to undertake such a mission, we are qualified for the assignment because each of us is, herself, a daughter of the Divine. With hearts, arms, eyes, and ears open we will know how the Divine yearns to love through us.

I am yours, Beloved, use me as an angel of love.

My heart and arms are open to myself and others.

Unfurling Our Wings

I'VE HEARD IT SAID THAT THE POWER WITHIN US doesn't wake up until *we* do. What does waking up mean? I believe waking up means that we women, individually and collectively, need to accept the reality that, when our wings are unfurled, we are powerful spiritual beings with a huge capacity for bringing healing to ourselves, one another, and our planet. A woman's wings naturally contain the nurturing feathers of inclusion, cooperation, acceptance, compassion, wisdom, intuition, and love—all qualities that our society needs in large measure.

If our own wings have been clipped by disrespect, dishonor, lack of opportunity, or mistreatment—and most women's have to a greater or lesser degree—then our first priority is to heal ourselves. To become an angel, we must, first, allow ourselves to heal in the embrace of angels.

Visualize yourself standing in a beautiful ray of sunshine. Before you is a full-length mirror in which you see yourself reflected wearing your spiritual wings. Examine them carefully. Can they freely and easily unfurl? If not, what do they need in order to soar as they were made to do? If you don't like the way they look or feel, change them. You are the artist; create wings that please you. Don't hesitate to ask for assistance in refurbishing your wings if you would like it. Practice unfurling your fabulous wings and, like a mother dove, spread them protectively over others.

Fortunately, we have guides along our spiritual paths who help us heal and are continually issuing wake-up calls that encourage us to unfurl our wings, empower ourselves, and live in harmony with our unique truth. Insights, flashes of intuition, and hunches are all nudges from inner or outer angels, urging us to wake up to and live from our unique wisdom. As we do, healing will take place.

Protecting ourselves and all of our Mother's children under the wings of love is our awesome mission, and we can accomplish it by simply being our true selves.

I fly on wings of love.
I am a powerful spiritual being.

Bearing the Light

WHILE WE ARE CONTINUALLY SURROUNDED BY the support and love of angels, we are also called upon to be Emissaries of the Light and intermediaries for the Divine in some situations. As White Eagle tells us, "You are a bearer of the Light, for you are as the Divine Mother, bearing within you the Light of the Son. Take the Light out into the world to bless and to heal, and quicken the vibrations of the whole earth." Our calls, which often come in the form of intuitive nudges and emotional hits, probably mean that someone is in need of our intercession and help.

One morning, I awoke suddenly at 4:45 A.M. with a foreboding feeling about my son. I've learned to pay attention to those intuitive prods and, knowing that he was taking part in the Baltimore Triathlon that day, surrounded him with light and prayed, "Mother/Father God, I ask that any negative circumstance that may befall Brett will be transformed and transmuted through love into the perfect, right experience," until I finally fell back to sleep around 7:30.

Sure enough, one of Brett's tires blew out during the bike race, but although he was in the middle of the pack, all of the other riders managed to avoid him. No one was hurt, thank God. It was very disappointing for him to go all that way and be disqualified, but it could have been much worse.

When you feel the urge to pray for someone, you can breathe them into your heart and then out into the care of their angels, or use the prayer I prayed for Brett, or repeat the Protection Prayer, which is: "The light of God surrounds you, the love of God enfolds you, the power of God protects you, and the presence of God watches over you. Wherever you are, God is," or whatever your wisdom guides you to do.

We bear the white light and ability to pray, which have the power to mitigate if not change circumstances.

I bear the light of the Divine Mother.

I listen to my intuitive nudges and act on them.

Being Our Own
Best Friends

*When one is a stranger to oneself then
one is estranged from others too.*

—*Anne Morrow Lindbergh*

THE ESSENCE OF OUR TRAINING AS WOMEN has been that we must sacrifice ourselves for others. In doing so we often lose the friendship of the one person who is always with us—ourselves. A friend provides us with vital ingredients for a satisfying life—support, appreciation, fun, understanding, and nourishment. A good friend acts as a gentle mirror, reflecting our strengths to us with congratulations and our weaknesses with tolerance. Without friendship our life is flat and our path toward authenticity extremely rocky.

If we have the idea that liking ourselves is selfish or egotistical, being a friend to ourself will necessitate a change in underlying beliefs. Change always requires courage. Committing to moving beyond devaluing ourselves to truly valuing ourselves is a life-affirming decision. Having ourselves as a trusted friend is essential for joy, growth, and healing. We can become a loving and supportive friend to ourselves—a person with whom we are delighted to spend our time.

Disrobing the Inner Judge

MANY OF US SEEM TO HAVE A NEED TO punish ourselves, and there are no light sentences. Our inner judges sentence us to hard labor in the frigid Siberia of guilt for the slightest infraction or mistake. Such treatment is incredibly hard on our hearts and spirits. Overcoming the tendency to be too hard on ourselves allows us to continue to call on the discernment of a wise inner guide without suffering inappropriately severe self-punishment.

As a teenager, Amanda used drugs rebelliously and had been promiscuous. As an adult, she was the model of decorum. She appeared calm and assured to those who knew her casually, but her family, especially her children, knew her perfectionism all too well. She needed to be in control— everything had to be done exactly as she dictated. Whenever her tight ship sprung even the smallest leak, she couldn't sleep or eat.

She was being eaten alive by unresolved guilt over her actions as a teenager. Firmly ensconced on the bench, her inner judge continuously banged her on the head with his gavel. Only by being totally in control of her surroundings could she silence him.

In order to transform a harsh judge into a loving

counselor and guide, we need to know what the judge is saying to us. When we are conscious of our judgmental voices, we can then choose different messages. Guilt and punishment foster fear. Tolerant and understanding messages foster learning.

Having the courage to disrobe our inner judge and lay aside the handcuffs of guilt allows us to be more tolerant and loving toward others also, which, in turn, draws more love to us.

I am a worthwhile and capable woman
even though I make mistakes.

I love and appreciate myself.

Tending Our Inner Garden

GARDENING IS A SOUL-FEEDING ACTIVITY FOR many of us. We nurture and care for our flowers, vegetables, and trees by watering, weeding and feeding them. Often we talk to them.

Studies done using special photography demonstrate that plants react differently depending on how they are spoken to. When addressed in a soft and soothing manner, the energy around a plant expands and brightens, and the plant leans toward the speaker. But when a plant is spoken to harshly or approached threateningly, its energy field constricts, the colors around it darken, and it leans away from the perceived threat.

What kind of gardener are we to our inner gardens? Do we cultivate kindly? Prune with patience? Encourage and appreciate our flowering and our ability to bear fruit? There is no other flower like us. We are each unique and beautiful, worthy of the finest care. A compassionate inner environment allows us to bloom more readily and more exquisitely.

Gently allow an image of a flower to come into your mind's eye. Imagine this flower is a part of you that is thirsty for appreciation and care. See yourself watering the flower from a beautiful pitcher. Imagine your flower lifting its head to accept the refreshing sprinkle. Feel its roots thankfully absorbing the sustaining and empowering water. Soak in the sensation of being nurtured and encouraged to grow.

I gently and courageously prune limiting beliefs and actions from my life.

I appreciate the unique beauty I bring to my world.

Empowering Ourselves
through Praise

. . . .

HOW MANY TIMES DO WE CONGRATULATE OUR-
selves? How many more times do we criticize ourselves? Congratulating is energizing; criticizing is
debilitating.

At the end of a therapy year, Meg lamented, "I
haven't accomplished anything all year long!"
From my perspective, she'd done amazing things
and healed in wonderful and courageous ways. To
help her change her habitual self-criticism, I gave
her a sheet of little gold stars and asked her to
make a list of her accomplishments for the year,
both inner and outer, and to give herself a star for
each.

When she came back the next week with the
list, she was amazed at how many stars she'd
been able to give herself. Having changed her self-
criticism to self-congratulations, her attitude was
entirely different. She laughed more easily and felt
excited, energized, and empowered.

Being a good friend to ourselves means that we
have the courage to stop crippling ourselves with
criticism and learn, instead, to compliment and
congratulate ourselves. We can make it a habit to

"gold-star" ourselves and become empowered through praise.

I congratulate myself for the good things
I do, say, and think.

I deserve gold stars.

Accepting the Beauty of
Our Imperfections

. . . .

IF WE INDULGE IN THE "COMPARISON CRUNCH," the victim is usually our self-esteem. There will always be someone smarter, thinner, more creative, prettier, or younger than we are. We're all filled with holes like Swiss cheese, but our inadequacies are in different places.

Being a recovering perfectionist, I have adopted as my motto the disclaimer often found on clothes made of cotton or raw silk. "This garment is made from 100 percent natural fibers. Any irregularity or variation is not to be considered defective. Imperfections enhance the beauty of the fabric."

What a great way to look at ourselves! Our imperfections enhance our beauty. Not that we don't want to change, grow, or do our best, but by celebrating the fact that we are made from "100 percent natural fibers," we create a climate of acceptance in which transformation can take place.

Close your eyes and imagine yourself as a unique and priceless tapestry created entirely from natural materials. Admire your tapestry exactly as it is now. Your wise subconscious has given you a rich symbol to explore. Write down your feelings and thoughts about your tapestry. Give thanks for its uniqueness, and appreciate it as is.

I accept myself just as I am now.
I give thanks for myself and my imperfections.

Waking Up to Self-Love

GENUINE SELF-LOVE IS VALUABLE, ALTHOUGH often rare. Self-love is not selfishness or egotism; rather it is the creation of a hospitable and supportive inner environment in which we can become our better selves.

The breakup of my first marriage was one of the most potent wake-up calls I've had in my life. Incredibly powerful, though painful, lessons came from my divorce. In my healing process, I realized I had lived with such self-condemnation that I had virtually made myself unlovable to others also. Wanting and needing love in my life, I made a commitment to start by loving myself.

Moving from a place of self-condemnation to self-love was a difficult process. It felt so unnatural to think of loving myself. But sticking with the commitment I made has reaped more benefits than I dreamt it would for me, my family, and my clients. Having the courage to open up to loving myself seemed to open my eyes to love that was always available to me but hidden from my sight because I felt unlovable.

The following exercise will be difficult for those of us who find the concept of self-love hard to understand or accept. Having the courage to overcome our discomfort and do it anyway can work miracles in our lives by creating a nurturing inner climate conducive to love, empowerment, and peace of mind.

Look at yourself in the mirror each morning and say, "I will be a good friend to you, (your name), today. I love you." Repeat each evening.

I am willing to love myself.

I love myself.

Receiving Validation

WOMEN ARE SO OFTEN TAUGHT TO BE modest and self-effacing that it is uncomfortable for us to be faced with validation. About a year after my first book was published I attended a seminar on writing. As we were introducing ourselves, another participant began to praise my book to the group. I was astounded at the array of feelings that assailed me as she spoke—gratitude, embarrassment, pride, intense fear, and the desire to Alice-in-Wonderland down the nearest crevice.

Like Alice, I felt painfully conspicuous, lost as to the proper facial expression or response. My body stiffened; my smile felt as if it were made from hardened wallpaper paste. I was terrified. Who was terrified? My inner teenager, who was saying, "Oh no! If they hear I am good at something, they will be jealous and not like me."

If intense feelings kick up for us in certain situations, we can help sort through them by asking ourselves, "Who is feeling this?" Then, being a good friend to that inner part of ourselves, we can ask her what she wants and needs from us right now and give it to her. In the writing seminar my inner teenager needed to be reassured that validation is not necessarily coupled with jealousy and rejection. She could be loved, accepted, and validated at the same time.

Being able to accept validation is to have the courage to be modest and self-effacing only when it is an authentic response. When we are successful, we can be fearless in accepting praise for the good job we have done.

I am a valuable and worthwhile person.

I deserve validation and praise.

Replenishing through Rest and Relaxation

· ·

FOR EACH OF US, THERE ARE A MILLION AND one real and imagined demands on our time and energy and so allowing ourselves the necessary rest and relaxation is often difficult. One of the best ways to befriend ourselves is to make sure we listen to our body, emotions, and spirit, and give ourselves the rest we need to revitalize and recharge.

Cars often have a helpful red light that blinks, alerting us to low fuel. And when we truly listen to ourselves, we can also hear the message, "Help! I'm running out of gas." We may hear the message and yet ignore it.

Being a good friend to ourselves means hearing and heeding the empty-tank message. We all need rest and relaxation, and we all deserve to rest and relax. In order to feel loving and be able to snap and crackle with energy, we need to give ourselves permission to snap, crackle, then plop.

Make a list of the activities and places that relax you. It may be taking a walk in nature, quietly listening to music, or doing nothing at all. Having the courage to not let the demands of others interfere with our special time is being a good friend to ourselves. We need to allow ourselves some time

each day to rest and relax in our own unique way.
Only we know when it is time to fill up our tank.

I deserve rest and relaxation.

*I take time to replenish my energy
through rest and relaxation.*

Discovering Our
Personal Diamond

KNOWING AND ACCEPTING THE VARIOUS
aspects of ourselves is sometimes difficult. There
are often slices we want to ignore or reject. Truly
accepting all parts of ourselves as they are provides
a climate in which transformation can take place.

One way to think of ourselves is as diamonds,
many-faceted and meant to reflect the light. We
are each special and unique diamonds. There are
no others like us. In being good friends to ourselves, we need to explore all of our facets, realistically appraising ourselves by looking at all aspects
of our being. Each facet, no matter how dark it may
seem, will reflect the light clearly when it is
cleansed of old wounds, beliefs, and patterns.
Celebrating the facets that are freely reflecting the
light of our higher selves, and gently beginning to
heal those that we have denied because they are
cloudy and obstructed, requires great patience and
courage from us.

To help internalize the symbol of yourself as a
diamond, gently close your eyes and imagine you
are at the edge of a lake. The surface is absolutely
calm, glasslike. A small point of light begins to
reflect off the water and soon becomes a beautiful,

shimmering brightness resembling thousands of brilliant diamonds dancing on the surface of the lake.

Visualize the light expanding to include you. Feel yourself and the entire lake as one big diamond reflecting light and love to all around you until it encompasses your family, friends, and finally the world as a whole.

I value myself as I would a precious diamond.

I gently explore all facets of my being and love each of them.

Asking for What We
Want and Need

WE KNOW HOW TO BE CARETAKERS, BUT CAN
we reach out when we need to be taken care of?
We women are proficient at giving, but receiving
often seems strange and, somehow, not right. Emotionally battered and bruised from my mother's
diagnosis of terminal cancer, I dragged myself to a
day-long workshop I'd signed up for before her illness. I was excited when an older woman intro-
duced herself as the author of one of my very
favorite books, a book that lifted my heart each
time I read it. Although feeling a kinship with the
woman and yearning to meet her, I held back
because I felt so drained—I was afraid she might be
turned off to me because I was in such pain.

Finally I said to myself, "Sue, how can you be a
good friend to yourself right now?" The answer
was clear, "Risk! Ask for what you want and need."
Hesitantly, I told her how important her book
was to me and asked if I could just sit by her side
and soak in her mother-energy since my own
mother was dying. Kindly, she answered, "I would
love to be your mother today." I spent most of the
day with my head in her lap. Having gathered up
my courage to ask for what I wanted, I received

more than I'd hoped for.

We all have the right to ask for what we want and need. Once we have the courage to ask, most people will feel privileged and gratified to help us in any way they can.

I deserve to have what I want and need.

I have the courage to ask for what I want and need.

Finding
Peace of Mind

"Where you tend a rose, my lad,
A thistle cannot grow."

—Frances Hodgson Burnett

UCH OF OUR DAILY LIFE SEEMS IN direct opposition to acquiring peace of mind. We are often busy, rushed, and over-committed, which keeps us out of balance and off center. Because the world seems to live without peace of mind—addicted to chaos, chemicals, and calamity—it is courageous for us to take a different path and say, "This is not for me."

Committing to moving toward peace of mind, no matter what the circumstance, is a constant struggle for many of us. In fact, we often believe that mental turmoil is the norm and serenity an unrealistic Pollyanna dream, but that is not true. Peace of mind is attainable. Serenity is possible. We can have them both; not always, but a good majority of the time. Having the courage and strength to insert quiet time into our schedules and change disturbing thought patterns and beliefs to life-affirming ones is a gift we have the power to give ourselves.

Pausing in the Oasis of Silence

WITH OUR FAST-LANE EXISTENCE IT IS EASY to neglect quiet time, to feel there are more important things to do. But it is in the quiet that we are replenished, renewed, and recharged for the demands of our lives. In silence we can reconnect with our true source of energy and inner wisdom. The "still, small voice" is heard more in the silence beyond, around, and beneath language than it is in the cacophony of incessant sound.

As much as our physical body needs water in order to live, we need silence in order to have a rich emotional and spiritual life. To illustrate the importance of silence to the soul, we can recall a time when we were very thirsty and longed for the relief of a cool drink of water. In the same way, our souls yearn for the refreshing relief of silence.

Because lives focused on outward activity rather than inner contemplation seem more socially acceptable, it takes courage to have the self-discipline to pause each day in the oasis of silence. However, it is important that we persevere—for in quiet solitude, listening only to the sounds of ourselves, we can begin to hear the whispers and urgings of our own inner guidance.

Only in the oasis of silence can we drink deeply from our inner cup of wisdom.

I take time to experience the peace and serenity of silence.

I listen to and trust my inner wisdom.

Spending Our Moments
Wisely

. . . .

DO WE LIVE IN THE PRESENT OR, AS HUGH Prather says, "rehearse difficulties to come"? It's far too easy for many of us to fall into the trap of worrying about what may happen in the future or lamenting what happened in the past—neither of which do we have control over now.

Suppose someone gave us $1440 each day for the rest of our lives, but we had to spend all $1440 that day; none of it could be taken into the next. Each of us has been given something more priceless than dollars, 1440 minutes every day. Do we get our money's worth?

Living in the moment sounds good, but how do we learn to do it? Awareness is the key. We need to be aware of where our thoughts are, which means we need to have the strength to live consciously. When we discover our thoughts wandering back to the unchangeable past or forward into the unforeseeable future, we can choose to bring our awareness back to now, this moment.

Now is the only moment we truly have to live. Yesterday is irretrievable and tomorrow is unknown. Living in the moment is having the courage to live consciously, with awareness.

I savor each minute given me.
I appreciate each priceless day I live.

Cleansing Our
Emotional Bodies

JUST AS WE WASH OUR BODIES AND OUR clothes, we need to cleanse our emotional bodies. As we move through our days, many of us act as psychic garbage collectors vacuuming in other people's feelings. Women are especially prone to taking on everyone else's problems. The more sensitive we are, the more debris we collect. Since we have more than enough of our own baggage to deal with, it is essential we have the courage to let go of that which is not ours to carry. Cleansing our emotional bodies gives us the stamina and energy to begin another day.

In order to free ourselves from inappropriate feelings we have been subjected to during the day, it is wise to experientially symbolize purifying our emotional bodies.

One excellent way to do this is to take a shower or bath and, as you soak in or stand under the pouring water, imagine any limiting, defeating, and depressing feelings or beliefs being rinsed away. In as vivid a way as you can, see the emotions that are not yours swirling down the drain away from you. It is not your responsibility to shoulder them. Now visualize and feel the purifying water saturating the cleansed areas with love and energy.

I let go of feelings that are not mine.
I am full of love and energy.

Creating Peace of Mind through Forgiveness

. . . .

IT IS DIFFICULT TO CREATE A FLOW OF FORGIVE-
ness toward people with whom we are angry or
who we feel have wronged us. People whom we
have not forgiven have power over us—our
thoughts and our moods. When we forgive, we
free ourselves to have greater peace of mind.

At work Lillian supervised a woman whose main
goals in life seemed to be irritating her co-workers
and getting out of doing her share of the work.
The fact that bureaucratic loopholes made it
impossible for the woman to be fired caused Lillian
to arrive at the office each day a little more tense
than the day before.

She found the following exercise very helpful in
encouraging her heart to open, thereby diluting
the power she had allowed the woman to have
over her emotions. We all probably have someone
in our lives we could try it on.

Close your eyes and picture a person or thing
you love unconditionally. Your picture may be a
flower, a child, or a place—whatever or whoever
gives you the feeling of a full heart. See your heart
overflowing toward the loved object. Feel the flow
of energy toward the beloved. Take time to enjoy

feeling the expansion of your heart. Now, very gently, allow your original picture to fade and in its place bring the image of the troublesome person. Keep the loving flow going toward the new image. If you find it impossible to continue the flow, that's okay, just try it again at a later time. Eventually, you will be able to allow love to flow.

You do not need to feel affectionate toward the person, but in order to experience peace of mind, you do need to love him or her impersonally. Loving impersonally means you wish him or her well or, at least, wish them no harm.

Each day I am more and more able to love and forgive.

I allow love to flow through me to_____

Forgiving the Mother We Were

WE ARE SO VULNERABLE ABOUT OUR MOTHERING abilities. It's all too easy for us to feel guilty. Have we done too much or not done enough? Are we too strict or too permissive? Questions such as these can haunt us whether our children are fourteen days old or forty-seven years old. But in order to have peace of mind, we need to forgive the mother we were. This takes great courage, particularly in the face of society's attitude of "it-must-be-mother's-fault," no matter what "it" is.

When my first child was born, I was young, inexperienced, and unhappy—and not too great a mother. I wanted to be good, I tried to be good, but I wasn't the kind of good mother I eventually became.

Before I could relax and be the mother I wanted to be, I needed to forgive the struggling young mother I was originally. I did that by picturing myself in my early twenties, acknowledging my loneliness and confusion, and then assuring myself that I did the best I could at the time. And I had.

If you need to forgive the mother you were, allow yourself to close your eyes and see the young woman of the past. How does she feel, and how do you feel about her? Try to understand what motivated the actions or attitudes that you now need to forgive. Understanding fosters forgiveness.

We all do the best we can at the time. Knowing that helps us to forgive ourselves and, in a climate of forgiveness, we can become better than we were. If our relationships with our children are secure enough, after we heal our shame at not being a perfect parent, we may eventually want to talk to them about our regrets and ask for their forgiveness.

I forgive myself for my past mothering.
I lovingly support all children in my care.

Being Ourselves Today

AS WE COURAGEOUSLY WORK TO BECOME truly ourselves, each new day presents us with opportunities to unfold in the perfectly right way. A very wise woman once told me that "the future depends on a healed past and a well-lived present."

We create a fulfilling future, and honor our present, by living this day in a manner that will enable us to look back tomorrow with pride. Each day we can learn, from whatever sources inspire us, to love ourselves just as we are—unfinished and still struggling—and to live with our families, co-workers, and friends as a kind and considerate equal.

The talents, abilities, and idiosyncrasies we bring to this life are uniquely ours, and we are invited to share them with others in our own special way.

At the top of a sheet of paper write the heading, What Makes Me Unique? Then, writing as if you were your best friend, jot down several of your special attributes. For fun you might want to add a few quirks also.

We are one of a kind. Our individuality is a precious gift—a gift too sacred to be thrown away. It is our right, privilege, and responsibility to be ourselves today.

Today, I have the courage to be uniquely myself.
I give thanks for the gifts that I, alone, have to share.

Resting in Unseen Arms

. . . .

SO MUCH OF OUR ANXIETY AND INSECURITY comes from the deep fear that we are alone, adrift without guidance. It isn't so. We are uplifted and supported by many unseen, but present, friends and mentors.

One day during my mother's struggle with cancer, I was overcome with the frustration of living 1500 miles away, discouraged by our family's interactions, and bereft at the thought of losing her. At the point of collapse, I picked up a favorite little book, *The Quiet Mind*, and turned to a page at random. I read, "We know, Dear Child, how hard life can be, but we are ever with you." Seeing that sentence, I relaxed into a cleansing torrent of tears and had the most comforting feeling of being held. I didn't just think it, I truly felt nestled in the arms of someone who cared.

It was the words "Dear Child" that spoke to me since it was my inner little girl, soon to be motherless, who was inconsolable. My adult self, about to lose a friend, was not able to comfort the inner child as well as usual, so the thought and the feel of outside arms, ever near, was a balm.

Remembering to pause and ask for consolation, when we are in need, brings us calming peace of mind. Imagining ourselves in the loving embrace of

someone who unconditionally cares for us soothes
and quiets our quaking inner child.

I allow myself to rest in the unseen arms of God.
I am supported and loved by unseen friends and mentors.

Eliminating SHOULD, HAVE TO, *and* CAN'T

. . . .

ONE OF THE GREATEST HINDRANCES TO PEACE of mind is the way we talk to ourselves in the privacy of our own minds. As a therapist, I see many people who have a judgmental, parental voice inside that says, "You can't do it right. You didn't do enough. You should have known! You're wrong . . . you're bad." How would our house plants react if we talked to them the way we talk to ourselves? Would they wither or thrive? Would our friends trust and confide in us if we spoke to them the way we speak to ourselves?

Unfriendly self-talk causes great stress. We can eliminate at least thirty-five percent of our stress immediately by erasing the words SHOULD, HAVE TO, and CAN'T from our vocabulary. SHOULD, HAVE TO, and CAN'T are victim words. They imply we have no power, no choice. We can empower ourselves by replacing these victim words with CHOOSE TO, WANT TO, and WILL.

Because we have believed there are certain things we have to do, even more things we should do, and many things we can't do, it is very difficult to acknowledge that what our minds are telling us is not necessarily true. We simply don't have to, but we certainly may choose to do, think, or feel something.

Creating empowering self-talk is very simple—although not easy—and we're totally in charge of doing it. It starts with acknowledging that we have the power to decide to speak to ourselves in a positive way and then committing to do so.

I speak to myself in a loving manner.

I use empowering words such as choose to, want to, and will.

Imitating the Little Engine That Could

....

WHEN WE BELIEVE WE CAN'T, WE'RE RIGHT. When we believe we can, we are also right. Remember the children's book *The Little Engine That Could*? It's about a little engine who succeeded in pulling a train up a steep hill where other, larger, engines had failed. The little engine made it to the top because she kept repeating to herself, as she struggled, "I think I can, I think I can."

Tracy's mother read her the little engine book often because, as a child, she had the crippling habit of saying, "I can't." As an adult, like many of us, she sometimes regressed to that old pattern. One day, upon returning from a week out of town, she found herself feeling extremely stressed, almost paralyzed by the amount of work waiting for her. She tuned in to her inner dialogue and found she was repeating over and over, "I can't get all of this done. I have too much to do." Her subconscious was getting the message from those thoughts, "Red alert! It's time to panic!"

Becoming aware of her stress-inducing self-talk allowed her to change it to "I have all the time and energy I need to accomplish everything I want to do." She didn't believe it at first, but knowing the process does work, she kept repeating her new, empowering statement aloud. In the space of a few minutes, Tracy's body relaxed, her mind cleared, and she was able to work much more efficiently. And yes, she told me, everything eventually got done.

Although it takes tremendous courage to change old thought patterns, we can help ourselves do so by adopting the little engine's phrase, "I think I can, I think I can," when we feel helpless or overwhelmed. Keeping our self-talk empowering, not panic producing, helps us do what we want to do and enhances our peace of mind immeasurably.

*I have all the time I need to accomplish
everything I want to do.*

I can. I know I can.

Calming the Monkey-Mind

OUR THOUGHTS CAN BE LIKE A THOUSAND monkeys in a tree, swinging by their tails, arms, and legs from branch to branch, grabbing at each other and then whisking away. Monkey-thoughts especially love to dwell on fleas, those things that bug or irritate us—picking, scratching, biting at our minds until our feelings fester. It doesn't have to be so. We are in charge of our thoughts.

Because learning to be in charge of our minds is one of the most difficult and frustrating tasks we have, it is tempting to give up and remain at the mercy of limiting and fearful thoughts. It takes courage to persevere in taming our minds, but it is essential for our well-being. We need to believe with our whole hearts and minds that we can control what we think, and then practice that knowledge with diligence and patience.

So when we notice our monkey-mind concentrating on fleas, we can distract it with thoughts of bananas, love, or thankfulness. If the branch our thoughts are swinging from is perilous to our peace of mind, we can choose to jump to another more soothing one. We can decide what we allow our mind to concentrate on, but we need to be gentle with ourselves as we calm our monkey-mind, because doing so is a life-long process.

I choose to think healing, loving, and thankful thoughts.

*I have the power to create peaceful thoughts
even in stressful situations.*

Choosing "That's Good!"

NO MATTER WHAT HAPPENS IN OUR LIVES, WE have at least one choice. We can either say, "That's good!" or "Isn't it awful!" And the more we can say, "That's good," the happier we'll be because resistance magnifies pain, and labelling something as "bad" is resistance.

Polly, eight months pregnant with her fifth child, fell down an old-fashioned heating vent one day while her husband and children were away. Returning home six hours later, they found her wedged in the vent, calmly knitting. When she realized she couldn't get herself out, rather than struggling, crying, or worrying, she had chosen to make the most of a difficult situation by thinking how good it was her knitting was within reach rather than how bad it was that she was stuck.

Most of us would be hard pressed to be as sanguine as Polly in a similar predicament, but we can choose to see the good in most situations. It takes courage to resist feeling like "Poor little me" but making a commitment to ourselves to choose "That's good" is a giant step toward having peace of mind. When we notice ourselves resisting something that's happening to us and denouncing it as bad, we can stop and consciously choose a more positive reaction or attitude. Optimism and peace of mind go hand in hand.

I choose to look at things with a "That's good!" attitude.

I look on the bright side of situations.

Reprogramming Our Inner Mind

IF WE GET IN THE HABIT OF ALLOWING OUR subconscious mind to sabotage us by nastily flashing on to the screen of our consciousness statements such as, "Stupid! You did it wrong again!", peace of mind will elude us. None of us would buy a computer that did that to us. Rather, we would want a user-friendly machine that says, "Good try!"

Our minds are many times more fantastic than the very best computer and we are their only programmers. With strength, courage, and persistence we can change our negative self-talk to user-friendly inner dialogue.

Nyla's therapist asked her to keep a little notebook with her at all times and write down every time she spoke badly about herself. Being resistant to knowing exactly how hard she was on herself, it took every bit of Nyla's courage to agree to the suggestion. But she accepted the challenge and was amazed by how often she criticized herself; it took about a month of committed awareness and writing to extinguish her negative habit.

Changing a long-standing habit, such as negative self-talk, is difficult, so it is important we have ways to remind us of the desired new behavior. An excellent help would be to expand on Nyla's notebook exercise. Since our minds work similarly to computers, it is necessary to replace erroneous commands with correct ones in order to get the results we desire. Therefore, after jotting down the unfriendly remark made to ourselves, we need to write the corresponding positive statement—the statement we would like to habitually tell ourselves.

Immediately replacing a negative statement with a positive one is a powerful assistance in facilitating change. Peace of mind is a result of peaceful thoughts.

I speak to myself in a loving and supportive way.

I fill my mind with peaceful thoughts.

Avoiding the Future Hole

ONE OF THE QUICKEST WAYS TO DISTURB PEACE of mind is to worry about the future. I call this falling in the future hole. Future hole self-talk statements often begin with: "What if . . . ," "I couldn't handle it if . . . ," "I'm afraid that . . . " It's times like these when we need to remember the biblical observation: "Sufficient unto the day is the trouble therein." We can handle what comes our way today, but if we add what might happen tomorrow or two years from now we are seriously jeopardizing our peace of mind.

When Ginny suddenly found herself single after a long marriage, the hardest times she had were when she allowed her mind to project into the future. "What if I can't make any money?" "I couldn't handle it if my kids decided to live with their dad." "I'm afraid I'll always be alone." Falling in the future hole always landed her in the pits.

If we find ourselves worrying about the future, we need to pull our mind back to today, telling ourselves, "I can handle today, right now, this minute. Tomorrow is not here. Now is all I need to be concerned with." Gently bring your thoughts back to the now if they fall into the future hole again.

We need to plan for the future but not worry. Planning causes secure feelings; worrying causes pain. Planning is empowering; worrying is victim-izing.

I plan for the future but live in the now.
I trust my life (this situation) is unfolding
in the perfect, right way.

Keeping Afloat Through Forgiveness

....

LIFE JACKETS SAVE OUR LIVES BY SUPPORTING US when we are tossed into stormy seas and are just too tired to tread water. Without a life jacket many unfortunate sailors would drown before they could be rescued.

As we sail through life, we all encounter storms and feel engulfed by tides of emotion. Forgiveness, or an intention to forgive, is one of our most buoyant life jackets. Others will surely disappoint or hurt us on occasion, whether intentionally or unintentionally. And we will do the same to them. Having the courage and willingness to forgive our own and others' shortcomings is an unfailing life jacket—truly a life preserver—keeping us afloat.

Forgiveness is a process. First we need to feel and express our hurt, confusion, or anger constructively. When we are in the midst of externalizing our pain, we will not feel at all forgiving. That's perfectly okay and totally appropriate. However, it takes courage to resist the temptation to stay mad or hurt. At some point, for our own peace of mind, we need to forgive. Knowing our goal is forgiveness gives us support and direction as we move through and let go of difficult feelings.

As we navigate turbulent emotional waters, the intention to forgive is our ballast. Being unwilling to forgive is like a weight around our necks, submerging us even in the calmest seas. Forgiveness keeps us afloat.

I allow myself to express my pain constructively.

I have the courage to forgive myself and others.

Accepting the Unacceptable

. . . .

THERE ARE TIMES WHEN WE ARE CALLED UPON to have the courage to accept things that seem totally unacceptable—the death of a child, divorce, cancer, loss of a job, fire, and so on—and we wonder if we are strong enough to face it. Accepting tragedy is difficult and painful. And it is natural and even wise to rail against God or fate when we feel enraged and impotent, because that is part of the process of moving toward accepting the unacceptable. But in order to truly heal from an emotional, physical, or spiritual wound we need to stop resisting the fact that it happened. For resistance magnifies pain.

To help us accept the unacceptable, we can visualize life as an immense and magnificent tapestry. Having our nose pressed against the "Now" section of the pattern, we can't see the whole—and sometimes even the part—very clearly. When something happens that we feel is unacceptable, we can try to remind ourselves that at this close range we can't see how this fits into the pattern of our life and trust that, when we can step back and see the whole, this situation will somehow add to our growth and enhance the beauty of the entire tapestry.

Maybe we will never see the reason or the

A FRIEND OF MINE ATTENDING A CONference was surprised to notice that everyone at the breakfast table had coffee but her. She felt a little miffed and said, "Why didn't *I* get coffee?" Someone answered, "You have to turn your cup over, June, in order for them to pour you some." Ah, isn't that what we often do, forget to turn our cup up to receive?

Why do we often have such qualms about anticipating and accepting abundance? Maybe it's because historically we women rendered services that were largely taken for granted—rather than respected and reimbursed—and we learned to give to others but not expect anything for ourselves. In order to invite abundance into our lives we need to feel worthy of the myriad blessings life has to offer: supportive relationships, peace of mind, well-balanced kids, health, enough money, and satisfying work to name a few.

Whatever the reasons for our hesitancy in accepting all forms of prosperity into our lives, it is important *now* that we change any limiting beliefs and awake to the realization that we deserve to live abundant lives both practically and emotionally.

Flowing with the Current

HAVE YOU EVER GONE ON A RIVER-RAFTING TRIP? If you have, imagine what it would have been like if your guide thought it would be interesting to have you go *up* the river rather than down. The excitement of the trip would wane very quickly as you attempted the arduous task of fighting the current by going against the flow.

We wouldn't accept a guide like that, would we? But in our inner lives, so often we do just that! Daily our attitudes and beliefs about abundance launch us into the river of life and cause us to struggle upstream. If, for instance, we think that life is like a pie and there's not enough to go around, we will end up hungry. Or, if we believe that we deserve only a meager supply of respect, happiness, or dollars, that's probably what we will receive—which feels a lot like bucking the current.

Years ago, while taking a workshop on prosperity, a woman friend and I came face-to-face with limiting beliefs that kept us from entering the flow of abundance. We were asked to write down how much yearly income we wanted. While most of the men in the group blithely threw around figures with lots of zeros, Bonnie and I both came up with very conservative numbers. We worried about what others would think, wondered if we were deserving, and feared we wouldn't be loved and accepted if we had generous incomes.

We women need to uproot old self-denying beliefs about money and view prosperity as freedom—freedom to do more for ourselves and to be of better service to others. We need to encourage each other in learning to value our talent by accepting, as worthy, our ability to earn money.

When we believe that we are worthy to receive and that the universe benevolently wishes to give to us, we can flow *with* the stream of abundance and feel well cared for and wealthy no matter what the circumstances. Abundance is, in large part, an attitude.

I deserve to live abundantly.

Life is an abundant blessing and
I am worthy of every smidgen.

Setting Our Sails

. . . .

ONE OF THE MOST SUPPORTIVE THINGS WE
can learn to do for ourselves is to open up to
receiving what we want, need, and deserve. So
often we know we need to receive, but we don't
know how. We're very good at giving, but sometimes grapple blindly with the ability to take. We
move through our lives like a sailboat with its sails
tightly furled. The good news is that even the most
entrenched givers among us can invite abundance
into our lives by discovering how to set our sails so
that the wind can catch and fill them. But first we
must know that it is okay for us to get as well as to
give.

Toward that end, sit comfortably with your
back straight and begin to focus your attention
away from the activities of the day and toward an
awareness of the present moment only. If your
mind wanders, gently bring it back to the here and
now. If your body feels uncomfortable, rearrange it
in a better position. Quietly begin to think of
water—relaxing, soothing water. Allow the image
of a lake, ruffled by a gentle breeze, to come into
your mind's eye. Seeing that you are in a marina
filled with sailboats, you intuitively realize that you
know how to sail. Choose the boat that most
appeals to you and launch her into the lake.

Now become aware of what you want to do. Float? Row? If you prefer to sail, with great expertise and effortlessness visualize yourself unfurling the sails and setting them in the perfect way. Lean back on your cushions with your hand on the tiller and allow the wind to work for you. How does it feel to easily glide over the water, tacking to catch the optimum breezes? If it feels good, continue to enjoy the experience. If you are uncomfortable, gently allow yourself to move back to a place where you feel safe and secure and assure yourself that you deserve to receive all the good that you want.

Be gentle as you gain the confidence to accept from others as well as give to them. It's not easy to change, but through trust and self-support, we can come to really *know* that it is okay for us to open our sails.

I am able to receive easily and graciously.

*Love and light flow to and from me
in ever-increasing amounts.*

Aging Successfully

. . . .

WE OFTEN DREAD AGING, BUT IT CAN ACTUALLY bring with it our greatest sense of comfort and security. Author Jean Shinoda Bolen researched the times in women's lives when they felt the happiest. Her results were surprising: the happiest women were often those who lived alone and were between the ages of sixty and seventy. These women obviously knew how to age successfully.

It is possible for us to learn to enjoy aging by concentrating on the gains inherent in it rather than the losses. To help me focus on the positives as I age, I adopt a new motto each decade. In this decade, my credo is *Fifty is Freedom*. My fifties have brought me the freedom of no longer being chained to "What will *they* think?" but instead, "What do *I* think?" What a blessing and a relief! A wonderful compensation for swaying underarms.

To help you focus on the abundant advantages of aging, jot down some of the joys and freedoms you've gained from living as many years as you have. What lessons have you learned? What emotional chains have you loosened? What wounds have you healed? Take a moment to give thanks for these benefits of aging.

Calmly close your eyes and visualize yourself as a wise and peaceful old woman. See the woman you are today bestowing upon that venerable older you the respect she so richly deserves. Ask her what she wants and needs from you today to ensure that she will continue to age successfully. Are you willing to give her what she requests? If not, ask yourself why. What are you afraid of? If you can give your aged self what she needs, assure her of your willingness to do so and ask if she has any wisdom she would like to give you now. When you feel complete with this meeting, tenderly leave her, knowing that you can return to her side whenever you desire.

Gratitude for the abundance of experiences and wisdom we have accumulated through the years helps us to age successfully.

Each year I grow in wisdom and acceptance.
I am comfortable with the age I am now.

Pigging Out on Life

. . . .

AUNTIE MAME, THE QUEEN OF ABUNDANT living, tells her nephew, "Life is a banquet and some poor fools are starving to death!" in order to teach him to enjoy life to the fullest—to pig out on life. Unfortunately, that's not the message many of us interpreted from what we observed growing up.

Many of us carry into adulthood the vague feeling that abundance is somehow bad. Perhaps those ideas were spawned while learning to share our toys as children or were a misinterpretation of the oft-heard "Money is the root of all evil." Even though the Bible verse condemns the *love* of money, not money itself, we feel guilty pigging out on prosperity and settle for gumming life into a numbing blandness.

Even less fortunate than those of us who assumed from society that it is better to be deprived than privileged are those who were told directly that *they*, personally, were unworthy of privileges. I commented to my client Vanessa on how pretty her bracelet was and to my surprise tears sprang to her eyes.

Vanessa, an incest victim, had worn the bracelet on a visit to her parents' home, and her mother said, "Why do you think you deserve to spend that much money on something as frivolous as that?"

Needless to say, Vanessa was crushed and vowed that she would not wear the bracelet again until her wounded inner little girl was healed enough to understand her mother's warped attitude and strong enough not to take her put-downs so to heart. Vanessa's tears honored the pain she had endured as a child and the determination she had shown in moving beyond it. The bracelet had become her silver badge of courage.

To help us learn to pig out on life, we can adopt an inner Auntie Mame who unfailingly tells us that we're worthy of partaking of the banquet and no longer need to starve in the midst of plenty. As we begin to value ourselves as lovable, unique beings who have the right to live life to the fullest, we will grow in our ability to accept all the good available to us and believe that, as Julia Child says, "Life is the proper binge."

I am a unique and lovable woman.

I am free to pig out joyously when appropriate.

Kissing the Hand That Feeds Us

To feel as though we are living abundantly, the first thing to do is fall in love with ourselves—to kiss the hand that feeds us instead of snapping and snarling at it. I know that may sound narcissistic but it really isn't. Appreciating ourselves teaches others to treat us better and means that the person we are always with—ourself—is in our corner.

An experience I had at a restaurant gave me an amusing framework for the idea of kissing the hand that feeds us. The handsome and suave waiter graciously, and it seemed sincerely, referred to me as "Beautiful Lady" throughout the meal. He caringly laid the napkin in my lap, leapt to fill my water glass, and even rushed outside to tell me goodnight as I left. He *served* me during that all-too-short meal, and I felt cherished as the object of his chivalrous attention. His was the most generous tip I've ever given, and it was well worth it.

Later, as I was chuckling over the feelings I had during that dinner, I thought, What if we graciously and caringly waited on ourselves? What if we served ourselves in ways that made us feel special? What if we were solicitously aware of our needs and enthusiastically hastened to fill them? If we treated ourselves this well, might we not return that favorable treatment with liberal gratuities of increased confidence and an abiding sense of self-worth?

Give yourself the gift of a day in which you wait on yourself as my waiter did me. This does not mean that you necessarily change your routine, but for this one day—which, hopefully, will stretch into a lifetime—make it your joy and privilege to ask yourself, "What can I get you to make this day better? How may I serve you right now?" Learning to kiss the hand that feeds us means that it will gladly pat our cheek in return.

*I am a beautiful, unique being and
treat myself accordingly.*

*I joyfully fill my own needs and have the courage
to ask for what I want and need from others.*

Stoking the Fires of Creativity

. . . .

ELIZABETH BARRETT BROWNING ONCE SAID, "Light tomorrow with today!" That is great advice, and following it means we have to get fired up *today*, aflame with the desire to follow our dreams.

To fan the flames, we need to be enthusiastically supportive of our ideas, no matter how crazy or far-fetched they seem. We are *all* creative—we have only to tune in to our night dreams to verify that—but so many of us throw the cold water of "I can't do that" or "My ideas aren't *really* very good" onto our original notions. Dampened by doubt, the fires of creativity can fizzle. It's up to us to fan the flames of our own creativity. Believing in ourselves is the most powerful bellows we can use to kindle the fire of creative thought.

Another good way to help a tiny creative ember become a raging fire is to make it *fun!* Gather people around you who help you keep your ideas aflame by treating them respectfully, but *lightly*. When we take ourselves too seriously we dry up. But if we enjoy the process and excitedly brainstorm about our ideas, the creative juices flow.

In order to begin oiling your creative cogs, quickly, without really thinking, jot down at least six completions to this statement: If I believed in myself, I would _____. Just as quickly and nonjudgmentally finish this sentence: If I gave myself permission to follow my dreams, I would _____. Play with what your sentences tell you. Make up some of your own sentence starts and then finish them. Catch fire and play with the process.

You are creative! Dare to do new things. Stretch and risk. It is okay to try and fail. In fact, when we're truly creative, failure is an essential part of the process. The only true failure is not trying. We can tap into abundant creativity by believing in ourselves and getting fired up.

I believe in my own creativity.

I enjoy trying new things and having new ideas.

Becoming a Conduit of Grace

. . . .

THERE ARE PEOPLE WHO SEEM TO BE LIGHTNING rods for grace. From them flows an almost visible vibration of compassion, and to be around them is to feel blessed and uplifted. Some are saints and some are *ordinary* people who have the extraordinary ability to allow respect and kindness to flow through them—not all the time, but at least on occasion.

Several years ago I had the opportunity to watch someone become such a conduit. I was with Dr. Elisabeth Kübler-Ross when she went to see a patient. As we walked toward the young woman's room, Elisabeth was grousing about something and I remember thinking she was in an irritable mood.

Although an irritated doctor pushed open the door, a radiant, grace-filled, and compassionate woman walked into the room. I could only watch in awe as love emanated from Elisabeth to the beautiful quadriplegic lying on the bed. In the space of the few minutes we stayed, that hospital room was converted from a sad and impersonal last stop to a sanctuary of acceptance and peace.

I think that one of the reasons Elisabeth is such a wonderful conduit of grace is that she is totally committed to bringing peace and comfort to the dying and bereaved. Because her *intention* is absolutely clear, even in the midst of irritation, she can move into a centered place and allow healing energy to flow through her. If Elisabeth can do it, so can we.

Close your eyes and gently focus on your breathing, allowing it to move in and out naturally. For a few minutes think of nothing but your breath. Without effort, bring your mind back to your breath as it wanders off. Ask yourself what type of grace you would like to become the conduit for today. Visualize yourself walking through your day as though you already *were* such a conduit. How does it feel? Notice how your grace-giving affects the people you meet. Allow that grace to flow to you, through you to others, and return to you.

We can become a loving conduit for the grace that fits our particular journey.

I am a conduit of grace.
Loves flows to me and through me.

Flying with a Tailwind

ABUNDANCE COULD BE DESCRIBED AS THE knack of living in an attitude of gratitude. If we constantly run on fast forward, frantically trying to keep up with what *should* and *must* be done, without taking a break to restore ourselves and count our blessings, we'll soon run out of gas. Stopping for a rest, pausing to really see the wonder in our world, and making room for interludes of thankfulness helps give us the energy to keep going.

Gratitude is a tailwind that enables us to travel farther and faster. An elderly relative of my husband's is almost an invalid and yet has a joyous spirit. Many of her conversations begin with such statements as, "Isn't it wonderful that . . . ?" "Have you ever seen a more beautiful day?" and "I am so lucky to have such wonderful friends!" Of course she has her low times, but with the resilience of a super-ball, she bounces back into an attitude of gratitude.

The flip side of that optimism was the attitude of a woman I spoke with who has been a hospice volunteer for several years. I was astounded when she said, "I don't see *anything* good in *any* of this illness stuff." None of us is in love with disease and death, but how sad for this woman, *and* the families she was sent to serve, that she never found the roses among the thorns.

Give yourself the priceless gift of extricating yourself from the whirlwind for a few minutes and write down all the things, just within sight, for which you feel grateful. Expand your list to include people and circumstances out of sight. As a bonus, add to your list some intangibles—attitudes, experiences, philosophies, etc. Looking at your list, allow your heart to open in a flow of gratitude and appreciation. Visualize that flow of thankfulness enveloping you like an iridescent mist that reaches out to embrace all those with whom you come in contact.

Flying with a tailwind of gratitude helps us savor the effortless times and move more quickly through the turbulent times.

I am grateful for my life.
I appreciate life, both the chaff and the grain.

Soaring from the Empty Nest

. . . .

CONTRARY TO THE POPULAR OLD WIVES' TALE (old mothers' tale might be more apropos here), women are not always bereft at the emptying of the nest. Many, in fact, find it one of the most liberating and abundant times of life.

Of course there are exceptions. Women who have no interests of their own outside the family or have used their children as their only emotional support, or those of us who have never learned to think of our own needs without guilt, may well fall prey to depression as the children leave. Since we can look forward to about thirty post-children years, it's important we start now to ensure that those decades will be meaningful and fun.

If your children are still at home, sit quietly in a place where you will not be disturbed (the bathroom was sometimes my last bastion of privacy) and picture yourself as a mid-life woman in an adult-only household. If you feel anticipation and excitement, you're probably one of those who will easily soar from the empty nest. If the thought of no children at home is troublesome, ask yourself where you are stuck in the mothering process. What do you need to do in order to release your kids into their adulthood and yourself into your fertile mid-years and beyond?

BIRTH IS A MIRACULOUS AFFIRMATION OF our ability to trust the feminine. Don't women, after all, have the awe-inspiring power to accept and incorporate the masculine and, together, create life? I believe that fear of this wondrous power is at the root of our distrust of the feminine. What a responsibility to accept and support such power.

Even if we never give birth to a child, we regularly and naturally conceive, nurture, and birth life in ourselves and others through emotional support and love. Realizing that we carry the power and innate wisdom to generate spiritual, emotional, and physical life, we can have confidence in the feminine within, knowing that she is willing and able to create a balanced and harmonious life for us when we choose to listen to her perceptive counsel.

The Sacred Feminine, in her highest reality, embraces all, synthesizing the divergent and the similar, welcoming both the wounded and the wise to her breast. She honors the Whole and is wholly trustworthy.

Honoring the Feminine Way

....

WATER, THE MOST POWERFUL *AND* MOST yielding of the elements, symbolizes the feminine way: strong and never deterred from its goal of union with its source, yet adaptable and creative as to the means by which it arrives at its destination. The feminine way is the way of the heart, unfolding and blooming in concert with the natural flow of life.

I learned a meaningful lesson about honoring the feminine way from the actor Gary Busey. While rewinding my aerobics tape, I inadvertently tuned in to a television interview just in time to hear him discuss his near-death experience following a motorcycle accident. In a sincere and soft-spoken way, Gary described seeing an incredibly beautiful light from which three androgynous Beings lovingly told him that the greatest tragedy was not death but what dies in us as we live. When asked by the clearly skeptical interviewer how he had changed, Gary said, "I'm more process oriented—not so goal oriented—and I see more into the heart of people and situations." "Are you happier?" she inquired. "Absolutely! Definitely! No comparison!" was his immediate response.

In other words, Gary Busey was catapulted off his motorcycle into an experience in which he learned to honor his feminine nature. I was impressed by how self-confident and peaceful he appeared as a result.

Visualize yourself as water, strong and powerful yet yielding and adaptable. Explore where you are now and where you want to go as this body of water. Absorb the feminine attributes of the water until you feel as though you have become one with it. Relax in the awareness that, while there may be temporary dams, *nothing* permanently impedes your journey toward eventual union with your source. If the water you imagine doesn't feel right—either too powerful, meandering, frozen, or stagnant— change it. Envision exactly what you yearn for from your feminine way. What "water-ness" do you want to bring into your daily life to better express your femininity?

I honor and respect my femininity.
I am able to be strong and flexible.

Discovering the
Sand Dollar's Surprise

. . . .

WHEN WE SHAKE AN INTACT SAND DOLLAR, WE can hear a little rattle and know that some surprise remains hidden inside. Breaking open the shell reveals five delicate objects resembling doves or angels. If Mother Nature unfailingly endows the simple sand dollar with angels, can we not trust that she does the same with us?

Although the sand dollar is pretty when whole, it's even more miraculous when broken and able to share its surprise. That's a lot like us; although we may look good and function well, it often takes breaking free of old patterns for us to really uncover the marvels within us.

To facilitate the process of discovering our hidden treasures, we need to examine the areas around which we have built protective shells and uncover the fears that prompted our need for shielding. For instance, out of a fear of rejection, I used to hide my opinions if they disagreed with others'. Another woman I know camouflages her sensitivity and vulnerability with a smoke screen of caustic humor.

To help you break free, make a list of ways in which you protect yourself. What shells do you hide in? Following that, write a separate list of the fears that originally made you feel the need for protection. Choose one fear to concentrate on now, and gently close your eyes. Allow a picture of the woman or girl within, who holds that fear, to come into your mind's eye. As much as you can, accept and befriend her. If that's difficult, just be with her, asking that your acceptance of her grow each day. Over time, repeat this meditation with the other fears that have confined you, for by accepting the wounded parts of ourselves, we begin to melt their defenses.

We are all laden with gifts and talents yearning to be released in order for their blessings to fly free.

I am free to be authentically me.

I know that I have many gifts and talents to share.

Reawakening to Wonder

How conscious and awake are we? Do we savor the current moment or squander it in anticipation or dread of tomorrow? One of the reasons children are so good for us is that they remind us to be absolutely present in the here and now. Taking a walk with a small child reeducates us in the ability to give wonder-filled attention to whatever we focus on.

The feminine within resonates to the same miraculous music that children do. It loves beauty and relationships, and savors genuine connections with people, things, and experiences. Reawakening to wonder reconnects us to the childlike attributes of attention and appreciation. Events and feelings become special and sacred when framed in undivided attention. Life becomes a fully conscious experience when made up of moments when we are really *real* and truly *present*.

As an experiment in reawakening to wonder, imagine that you are three or four years old and explore your yard or a park for half an hour. If the weather doesn't permit outdoor exploration, take a toddler-walk around your own home. Pay attention to the textures and tidbits; feel and even taste objects so familiar that you may not have really seen them since you last dusted, if even then. Open completely to the moment and the adventures it presents. *Awake* to your surroundings. Lose yourself in the here and now. Encourage yourself to be *amazed* and awed by the simplest flower or bug. Close your eyes and "see" objects with your other senses. Enjoy and relish what your childlike feminine self longs to appreciate more often.

When we realize that life is too precious to sleep through and accept our need to make time for the magical minutiae, we will be honoring the feminine within and supporting our much neglected inner child's desire to be awake to wonder. All of life, even the difficulties, can more readily be perceived as miraculous and wonderful when we encourage ourselves to become wonder-full.

I stop and take time to appreciate life's little wonders.

I invite my wonder-filled inner child out to play.

Inviting Spirit Through

. . . .

SPIRIT NEEDS US. WE ARE THE OPENINGS through which She can express. As we dismantle our own roadblocks toward spirituality, we can become Spirit's avenues and freeways (as well as back roads and dogtrots), her messengers of love and acceptance.

Although it may seem paradoxical, one of the biggest obstacles blocking Spirit from working through us is our own lack of self-love. Spirit can move only through a channel that, at some deep level, knows itself worthy and capable of such a mission.

The feminine within bears an intuitive flame that illumines awareness of our innate worthiness. Only as we come to listen to our wise feminine nature can we accept Spirit's commission to use us as a gateway for good.

Relax in a comfortable, quiet place where you will not be disturbed. For the first few minutes concentrate on your breathing, using as a prayer or mantra the words *opening* as you inhale and *to spirit* as you exhale. Very gently visualize a serene environment that you intuitively know is a place of sacred learning for you. Then confidently, without undue effort, invite a symbol of Spirit to join you. If you don't feel totally comfortable with the image that appears, it's not the appropriate one. Have it vanish, and ask for the right symbol to emerge.

When you are satisfied with your symbol, rest in its presence. Soak in its unconditional love. As you become more trusting of your Spirit, present to it one of the more shadowy sides of yourself, a part that shames or irritates you. Allow Spirit to minister to this dark aspect, bathing it in the light of unconditional recognition. As much as you can, open up to seeing the good buried in this aspect of yourself and, thereby, facilitate its transformation. Then bid goodbye to your Spirit, knowing that She is always available to you.

We are facets of the Whole, splinters of the Divine, through which the light of Spirit longs to shine.

I am worthy of allowing Spirit to flow through me.
I am a facet of the Divine through which loves flows.

Owning Our Inheritance

. . . .

WE ARE DAUGHTERS OF LIFE'S GENEROSITY, constantly surrounded by the altruism of Mother Earth and the myriad blessings present in work and relationships. It is our birthright to joyously claim this bountiful inheritance. Katherine Mansfield summed up her appreciative attitude beautifully when she said, "Life never becomes a habit to me. It's always a marvel."

One of the major keys to owning our legacy of good is to first appreciate all that we have and are privileged to enjoy now. Because feminine nature excels at appreciation, once we focus our attention in that direction, we can trust that it will flow naturally.

Of course there will always be difficult and painful things that we don't appreciate, but if we become so absorbed in them that we're blind to our blessings, our inheritance remains unclaimed and our lives seem gray and impoverished. Unlike sponges, we are in charge of what we soak up. We can choose to saturate ourselves with "Ain't it awful!" or we can overflow with gratitude and appreciation. Concentrating on the gold nuggets life offers, rather than the lumps of coal, gives us the feeling of being a beloved child, not an abandoned orphan.

Gently and without judgment, examine your outlook. Honestly take stock of your attitude. Is life a marvel or a hassle? Do you see the dust in a shaft of sunlight or feel its warmth? Are most people friendly and accepting, or are they out to get you? Do you appreciate your inheritance—all the varied physical, emotional, mental, and spiritual affluence—by counting your blessings, or do you reject it by centering on your *mis*fortunes?

Take a moment to visualize yourself in a beautiful gallery and begin to fill it with a display of your personal blessings. Maybe your array will include supportive relationships, good health, spiritual beliefs, satisfying work, gorgeous flowers, favorite books, uplifting ideas, peace of mind, and trust in yourself. As you carefully create your treasure trove, do so with thankful appreciation for your vast inheritance.

Life is always a marvel to me.
I am thankful for Life's gifts.

Wising Up

. . . .

IT'S TRUE THAT WISDOM COMES FROM MAKING mistakes and learning from them. The try-fail-succeed triune certainly does encourage us to increase our understanding of what is true, right, and lasting; but we also have an innate wisdom that we often fail to trust. One of the most powerful ways we can wise up is to acknowledge and act on that small, sagacious voice within.

It has taken me a long time to trust my own inner wisdom, and a large part of my journey toward self-love has included learning to listen and forgiving myself for not always honoring what I intuitively *knew*. One of my most dramatic denials came as I was walking down the aisle on my first wedding day. An interior sage was warning, "This is not right . . . I don't know why, but I know it isn't." I spent the next twelve years doing everything humanly possible to prove myself wrong, but we divorced anyway. I had *known*, but I had not listened.

Take a few self-supportive minutes to sit in a comfortable place and gently close your eyes. In concert with your breath, repeat the simple but profound sentence: I know. Continue this for a few minutes. If you notice you're thinking something else, easily return to *I know*.

In the landscape of your mind, see yourself in a lush meadow at the base of a mountain. Enjoy the sights and smells until the sound of water draws you up the mountainside. After an effortless climb you reach a level spot where a clear, steady spring is flowing from the mountain into a crystal pool. Feeling comfortable and at home there, stop and savor the freshness of the air and water. Drink from the spring, and as you do, realize that within you is a comparable fountain of wisdom. Ever flowing, ever clear, ever wise. Accept the awareness of your wellspring of wisdom, honoring it through trust.

We know! As we have the courage to open to and sincerely trust our feminine within, *woman* and *wise* will become synonymous—a matched set.

I trust my inner wisdom.

Each day I am more aware of my inner sage.

Reclaiming the Crone

. . . .

PROBABLY OUR ANCIENT ANCESTORS WERE much more sanguine about aging than we are because they revered the virtues that come with years and experience. Such cultures divided female development into three phases: maiden, mother, and crone.

The crone was wisdom personified. Ancient people saw, in woman's ability to bear children, their own bond to the sacred cycle of life and death. They believed that a woman withheld her menstrual blood to create a baby—life. As her menses stopped with the onset of menopause, they believed that a woman now held back the menstrual blood to birth wisdom. The crone's task was to embrace her wisdom, expand her creativity, and share, especially with other women, the knowledge she had gleaned from her years of experience.

Our foremothers and fathers respected crones and relied upon their counsel and guidance. Following their lead, we need to reclaim that respect *within* ourselves. When we can accept and respect our own creativity and wisdom on a deep level, others will naturally begin to view us as worthy of respect.

Turning fifty was a huge milestone for me. I committed myself to the belief that I had at least one foot in the Wisdom Ring; and when I slip into doubt, as I still do of course, I try to quickly remind myself of my years of experience and my commitment to owning my own excellence. If I can't sustain support for myself, I call in the cavalry by talking to friends who I know believe in me *and* are also dedicated to reclaiming their crone. As a light-hearted reminder, I have cards tacked around the house that say, *Caution, Crone Crossing!*

It's been said that in youth we learn and in age we understand. We can mine the gold of our years of experience by trusting that we have a vast store-house of wisdom that we are invited to share with others. With that understanding will come the reclamation of our crone in her highest form.

I embrace my wisdom and share it with others.

I respect myself and the wisdom I have gleaned from experience.

Completing the Circle

··

WE WOMEN CARRY THE FEMININE ENERGY OF the world. It is our task to honor the feminine in ourselves and insist it be honored in others and by others. We need to welcome, as our sacred duty, the task of bringing forth, from the shadows of obscurity, the feminine principles of kindness, consideration, and reverence in our personal lives and on our planet, so that we all can move from competition and chaos to cooperation and compassion.

It is our calling to complete the sacred circle of support by accepting blessings and *becoming* a blessing. Culturally and socially we have been trained to give to others, but in order to be an integral and constructive cog in the wheel of life, we must first complete the sacred circle within ourselves—feeding *ourselves* the feminine fruits of kindness, consideration, and reverence. From a vessel filled with such fruits, we'll be able to freely pour our best into the Whole, giving God and Her children the bountiful harvest of our love.

Because preparing ourselves to complete the circle is a sacred charge, reverently ask yourself what kind of blessing you would like to become. Are you already blessing *yourself* in that way? If not, what do you need to do in order to complete your inner circle? What attitudes would you like to change about yourself? What wounds need healing? What compassion do you need to show yourself? What fruits do you need to trustfully place in your vessel?

Like a pebble tossed in a pond, as we complete our inner circle by becoming a blessing to ourselves, circles of blessings will emanate from us to include countless others.

I give to myself as I give to others.

I am an essential part of the blessed circle of giving and receiving.

Embracing the Consort

HARMONY IN OUR LIVES IS SOMETHING WE all yearn for and work toward. But for this to happen we must first balance our dual inner nature, creating an intimate partnership of equals between the feminine and masculine energies in us—a sacred marriage that gives birth to the whole person.

Because society has enshrined the masculine by declaring it the *right* way to be in our world, we may first need to dethrone our masculine energy by empowering and honoring our feminine within, encouraging her to be our most potent inner influence. When we're strong enough to embrace, but not be overwhelmed by, our left-brain consort of male energy, femininity and masculinity can share the throne of our hearts, generating a synthesis between the differing, but equally valuable, aspects of our beings.

Barbara, an incest survivor, was having difficulty balancing her masculine and feminine energies. She vacillated between living totally in her feelings and being stoically rigid and controlling. It was an emotional roller coaster that caused her both emotional and practical difficulties. A series of dreams in which she gave birth to baby boys and felt unbounded love as she nursed and nurtured them helped Barbara heal the fear of men that she carried from her childhood trauma.

Through the dreams presented by her wise subconscious, Barbara realized that there was a deep part of her that was untouched by her frightening experiences with men, an aspect of herself that welcomed and trusted both the masculine and feminine energies. From that base of inner awareness, Barbara began to balance and harmonize her masculine and feminine within.

Like Barbara, we can tune in to our male and female selves and bring them into balance. Calling up and listening to the masculine and feminine aspects of ourselves lets us know if we have resistance to either energy. If there is quite a bit, I strongly suggest you find a therapist or friend who can help you trust and accept both the queen and the consort within.

I embrace my masculine energy with love and acceptance.

I am balanced and harmonized within myself.

Respecting Our Initiations

AT LEAST TWO ELEMENTS ARE ALWAYS PRESENT in initiation rites: an emotional and/or physical challenge, and the summons to let go of the old and move into the new. Because our psyches naturally move toward growth and wholeness, we constantly support our evolution by inviting initiation into our lives, whether we are conscious of doing so or not. Moving out on our own, making a living, falling in love, getting married, having a baby, being ill or caring for someone who is ill, surviving the death of someone we love are all initiations that both wound and renew us. Each of these initiations asks us to change, evolve, mature, grow up, and become the best that we can be.

If we're dragged kicking and screaming to an initiation, viewing it as an arbitrary happening over which we have no power, we've probably misunderstood our innate drive toward wholeness and will undoubtedly miss the invaluable learning intrinsic in it.

None of us eagerly hails growth that entails emotional or physical pain, but viewing our initiations as opportunities to become a wiser and more compassionate woman helps us feel less like victims and more like students. Being committed to learning as much as we can in our lifetime allows us to become a wounded healer whose empathy and understanding are the foundation of her healing energy. Perceiving our initiations as sacred rites of passage into the next dimension of our development helps us understand that from the blood of our initiation wounds can flow increased compassion, wisdom, and personal empowerment.

Trusting our innate wisdom, especially in the face of difficult initiations that rip us from people or circumstances we love, is a very powerful and necessary way to emotionally support ourselves. Opening to *all* of life's experiences empowers our intuition to become a wise inner sovereign, choosing well what lessons we learn.

Respecting our initiations and trusting the teachings that they bestow will bring us into communion with the collective wisdom and closer to wholeness within ourselves.

I accept and learn from the initiations life presents.

I trust myself to grow through the pain of initiation.

Gathering the Harvest of Maturity

. . . .

THERE ARE MANY BLESSINGS TO BE HARVES-
ted as we mature and ripen within ourselves: peace
of mind, flexibility, trust, and acceptance, to name
a few. As we develop, we often come into our own
power and stop spending time, energy, and money
on things that no longer satisfy us. Carl Jung, the
eminent Swiss psychologist, believed that our natural ability to do what we choose rather than what
we're told to do strongly emerges during maturity,
often after being *sub*merged for many years. What
a harvest that could be.

Although age is not the only determining factor,
the myriad experiences we have as a result of aging
do offer us many chances to ripen into maturity. I
have heard it said that when Sleeping Beauty wakes
up she is almost fifty years old. The writer M.C.
Richards has a wonderful view on Sleeping Beauty's
wake-up call: "The old saying that life begins at
forty has its basis in fact. For in maturity occurs a
natural birth of a selfhood which has been growing
within the womb of spirit. The generative principle
never ceases. It was a long time before I felt reborn
within myself the intuitions natural to childhood,
when freedom is a loyalty to life."

Freedom is a loyalty to life. What a profound observation. And who could be better at being loyal to

life than women, who actually have the capacity to birth life from their own bodies? The feminine within all women is aware of the cycle of life at a primal and cellular level. We *know*, we *wait*, we *trust*. We are attuned to the earth, moon, and sun because of our own cyclic nature, just as Mother Nature is attuned to her own sowing, growing, and harvesting cycle. What a natural jump for us, then, to become attuned to and grateful for the aging cycle of our life that brings with it increased freedom and maturity.

I happily gather the harvest of my maturity.

I choose to do what feels right for me.

Leaving White Space

· ·

WHEN WE OPEN OUR DAILY CALENDARS, how much white space do we see? Do we have blocks of unscheduled time or is our calendar filled to overflowing with commitments, committees, and appointments? Without white space in which to relax and be, we become overstimulated and sometimes even addicted to intensity—like a shark, constantly moving even in sleep.

We women have the abilities of a master juggler. We can survive while keeping a heroic number of balls in the air, but do we really thrive while doing so? Yes, if we also make room for plenty of silence in which meaning and wisdom can truly bloom. Blessings flow to us when nurtured in refreshing solitude.

Solitude gives us the opportunity to know what we feel and know what we know. Anne Morrow Lindbergh underscores that thought in *Gift from the Sea* when she says, "For it is only framed in space that beauty blooms. Only in space are events and objects and people unique and significant—and therefore beautiful."

In order to grow emotionally and spiritually, we must make white space a priority. It is in the privacy of white space that our hearts heal and expand. In the quiet of white space we can hear the urgings of our higher selves and receive the mysterious teachings from the feminine within. Framing our lives with intervals of contemplation and solitude gives us a better sense of self and greater peace of mind. Bringing these attributes into our daily life blesses not only ourselves but also those with whom we relate.

As an experiment, give yourself permission to take ten minutes a day just for you—ten minutes of solitude and silence. Make no demands upon yourself about how to "use" the time; just relax and be quiet. As you can, extend your solitary times. Although other time demands will be noisier, give yourself the spirit-enhancing gift of listening to the call from your higher self for white space, and rest and become revitalized in the silence. We can reap the benefits of solitude now.

I leave white space just for me.

I give myself permission to reap the blessings of solitude.

Transforming Archetypal Fears

. . . .

WE WOMEN ARE QUESTING FOR A DEFINITION of the feminine that's relevant for us today. In our search, we're reviewing how the feminine has been viewed in the past, and we are uprooting individual and collective fears about what it might mean for us to truly energize and utilize our feminine power.

Many of our fears are grounded in fact. Historians tell us that in the three years of the Spanish Inquisition nine million women were burned as witches. Later, in our own country, the same fate befell many women in New England. In general, these gender holocausts were perpetrated against women who were sought after for their healing, counseling, and midwifery skills. Their knowledge and wisdom—and in some cases, eccentricity—was perceived as a threat to the "powers that be" and so they were destroyed.

Is it any wonder that we hesitate to trust and empower our feminine nature? Embedded in our history are two messages: *wisdom is punishable by death*, and *to be fully empowered is to be life-threateningly vulnerable*. Our subconscious response to this is often fear of bucking the establishment, whether the establishment is the men in our lives, our bosses, our government, or even our own children.

What the executioners began with their witch

burnings, we have perpetuated through our unexamined personal and archetypal fears. We are
changing that, but we still need to transform any
ancient fears that continue to lurk in the shadows
of our subconscious. Only by bringing these fears
into the light, where they can be examined for
their present-day validity, will we transform them.

I am safe and protected.
I am wise and empowered.

Welcoming Our Angels

WRESTLING WITH OUR DEMONS IS SIMPLE AND often feels more appropriate than embracing our angels. We seem determined to invite into the ring of our life the demons of self-deprecation and disbelief, allowing them to throw us to the mat with alarming regularity. It's a different story when our angels—such as wisdom and intuition—come calling. We can't believe that they are real or that we are worthy of entertaining them.

One of the main reasons it's so much easier to acknowledge our demons is that we've been taught to trust them. Other people will affirm their existence with such statements as, "That's a dumb idea!" or "You're crazy." We learn to accept that we're not smart or worthwhile, and we then welcome representatives of our lower selves, our demons, into our belief systems because of their familiarity.

Angels, on the other hand, are emissaries of our higher selves, the essence of our beings, a distillation of our experience and innate knowledge. They are real, and we need to give ourselves the gift of learning to accept and trust their presence instead of denying and wrestling with them each time they appear.

Allow yourself to become quiet and centered, stilling your mind to the best of your ability. Imagine that you are seated in the midst of a soft, warm light. Feel it being absorbed into your body and your being. At the edge of the light stands an angel of intuition as well as a demon of self-doubt. Familiarize yourself with both of these visitors and then firmly insist that self-doubt fade away. Summon your angel of intuition to share the warmth and softness of the light with you. Open yourself in welcome to this symbol of your intuitive inner femininity.

We owe it to ourselves and those with whom we're in relationship to honor the wise and wonderful feminine within by accepting the aspects of our higher selves and acting in accordance with their principles.

I encourage myself to believe in my higher qualities.

*I welcome my angels of intuition and wisdom
into my awareness.*

Wielding Soft Power

. . . .

I FIRST HEARD THE TERM *SOFT POWER* FROM A wise young herbalist who is a scholar of the feminine mysteries. Although she often works ceremonially with young girls about to begin their menses, I met Gina at a fiftieth birthday celebration where she led us in blessing this woman's transition from mother to crone. I was touched by Gina's message of the potency, grace, wisdom, and responsibility of owning our feminine power in its highest form.

True feminine power is soft, meant to feed and heal ourselves, others, and our planet. I am reminded of our breasts with which we comfort and feed our children. Ideally we, ourselves, are like breasts—soft yet strong, beautiful and miraculous, able to provide pleasure as well as sustenance. As we women move from the discomfort of denying and being denied our personal power, to the supportive place of accepting and using it, we need to hold the highest conception of this power forever at the forefront of our minds.

Find a candle that symbolizes the feminine to you. At a time when you are confident of not being disturbed, light your candle and concentrate on the flame. As you rest in the glow, invite into your circle of light a female symbol for your feminine power in its highest expression.

If the symbol that first appears doesn't feel loving and supportive, invite it to leave. Once again focus on your candle flame and, when you feel ready, issue the invitation again. Become acquainted with the symbol of your feminine power, and bask in her wisdom. Ask her help in consistently and lovingly wielding your genuine, soft power. At the completion of your time together, she has a gift for you. Accept it with the full awareness that you are worthy of receiving it. Hold her gift, as a blessing and affirmation of your own soft empowerment, close to your heart.

Remember a woman's power is restorative, not destructive. With genuine feminine power, we can rebuild, replenish, and renew that which has been depleted.

I accept and embrace my soft feminine power.
I dedicate my power to the expansion of love.

Lighting Our Flame

. . . .

WHILE MEDITATING ON THE FLAME OF A candle floating in an iridescent, crystal wine glass, I was struck by the similarity of this candle to the potential we all have floating within us. Spiritual promise, our own unique light source, lies waiting to catch fire. We hold the matches, and it's our choice whether we light our interior candle or leave it floating coolly in the shadows.

Our spiritual potential will wait, for it is eternal. But would we not be warmer and happier—more our authentic selves—if we moved through the necessities, joys, and sorrows of our days warmed by the glow of this inner fire?

While contemplating the floating candle, one important thing I noticed was that the imperfections in the crystal showed up more clearly when the candle was burning than they did when it was cold. Maybe the defects amplified by the candle-light are symbolic of the fact that, even when we ignite our flame and consciously travel the path to enlightenment, we will not be perfect. Nor do we need to be. *But,* by lighting our inner flame, we *will* cast out darkness.

Settle in a comfortable, dark place and light a candle, quietly observing how far the light from this single candle travels. Notice the softness of objects illumined by it. As your breath deepens, gently allow your eyes to float closed. Without effort imagine yourself seated in front of a small bonfire. Well-being permeates your senses as you feel the warmth from the crackling flames. Looking down you see an exquisite candle lying on a velvet cloak and you intuitively know that these gifts are for you. Lighting the candle from the original fire, wrap yourself securely in the cloak and allow yourself to rest there, being renewed by your magical candle. When it feels appropriate to you, gently and carefully return to the present, knowing that the flame you carry is eternal.

Consciously lighting our spiritual flame means that we can more genuinely provide the warmth and comfort of illumined love both to ourselves and others.

I am a spiritual being.
I have a radiant inner life.

Seeing the Friendly Face of God

. . . .

HOW MANY OF US, AS LITTLE GIRLS, BELIEVED that God was a man? Well, that may have been okay if all the men we knew were loving and kind, but if they were not, our view of God was diminished and tainted. I don't pretend to really *know* what God is like, but my heart resonates with the idea that God is way too immense for us to possibly imagine. I believe that God incorporates all the wonderful qualities inherent in both women and men, as well as countless other attributes beyond our capacity to understand.

I wonder if God really cares how we view Her/Him/It as long as the face we turn to for comfort, love, and guidance is a *friendly* one. I like to believe that God wishes we felt able to safely and trustingly rest in Its Divine, Mysterious Presence.

Our need for spiritual connection is greater, even, than our need for interpersonal connection. But we can unite at a heart level with only a loving and friendly God, not a fearful one. Give yourself the priceless gift of exploring your current relationship to God. If your connection with the Divine is close, loving, and friendly, that's wonderful, and I'm sure your life is an inspirational light to others. But, if you'd like to see a friendlier face when you think of God, begin by exploring your most firmly held inner beliefs. Do you feel worthy of loving attention from God? Do you fear or resist the idea of a God? When you try to conjure up an image of God, what does it look like? What would it take for you and God to be *friends?*

The friendliest face of God lives in our inner temple of genuine self-love and acceptance. When we can befriend ourselves, we will more than likely be able to let God befriend us, also. From that sacred space, God can move through us and, in grace, bless all those who cross our path.

I am worthy of God's love.
God is love, and so am I.

Acknowledgments

AS ALWAYS, I AM DEEPLY THANKFUL TO THE wonderful people at Conari Press who, by their support and professional expertise, make it possible for me to bring my passion for writing to fruition. Special thanks to Brenda Knight, who is a goddess of intuition and conceived the idea of *Soul,* to Mary Jane Ryan who edits with flair and gentleness, to Laura Marceau who puts it all together with unfailing aloha, and to Jennifer Brontsema who magically crafts the pages.

Thanks from the bottom of my heart to my family, Genem, Mike, Brett, Lynnie, Paige, Shawn, Josh and Max, who provide much needed grounding and also heartily appreciated laughs. What in the world would I do without you?

Words cannot express the gratitude I feel for my women friends. Your love, wisdom, and encouragement not only bolster my spirits during the low times and soar with me during the high ones, but also help shape the person I am and the one I hope to become.

And special thanks to Auntie Es, an angel in disguise.

Sue Patton Thoele

Psychotherapist Sue Patton Thoele is the author of
THE COURAGE TO BE YOURSELF, THE WOMAN'S
BOOK OF CONFIDENCE, THE WOMAN'S BOOK OF
COURAGE, THE WOMAN'S BOOK OF SPIRIT,
AUTUMN OF THE SPRING CHICKEN, and HEART
CENTERED MARRIAGE. She and her husband, Gene,
live in Boulder, Colorado, and have four adult chil-
dren, a son-in-law, and one grandson. Sue has
recently become captivated by swimming with free
dolphins.

Conari Press, established in 1987, publishes books on topics ranging from psychology, spirituality, and women's history to sexuality, parenting, and personal growth. Our main goal is to publish quality books that will make a difference in people's lives—both how we feel about ourselves and how we relate to one another.

Our readers are our most important resource, and we value your input, suggestions, and ideas. We'd love to hear from you—after all, we are publishing books for you!

To request our latest book catalog, or to be added to our mailing list, please contact:

CONARI PRESS

2550 Ninth Street, Suite 101
Berkeley, California 94710-2551
TEL: 800-685-9595 • FAX: 510-649-7190
E-MAIL: Conaripub@aol.com
WEB SITE: http://www.readersndex.com/conari/